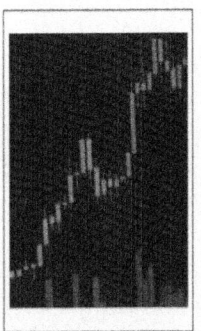

LET'S TALK ABOUT

FOREX TRADING

A COMPLETE BEGINNER'S
GUIDE TO TRADING THE
FINANCIAL MARKET

WWW.JEIVESTOR.COM

Disclaimer

The information contained in this book is for general informational purposes only. The author and publisher of this book have made every effort to ensure that the information contained in this book is accurate and up to date at the time of publication. However, they make no representations or warranties of any kind, express or implied, about the completeness, accuracy, reliability, suitability, or availability of the information contained in this book for any purpose.

The information contained in this book is not intended to provide financial or investment advice. The author and publisher of this book are not financial advisors, and the information contained in this book is not intended as a substitute for professional financial or investment advice. You should not rely on the information in this book as a basis for making any investment or financial decisions.

Forex trading is a high-risk activity, and there is a risk of losing your entire investment. The author and publisher of this book do not guarantee the success of any trading strategy or technique described in this book, and they are not responsible for any losses that may result from the use of such strategies or techniques.

The information contained in this book is subject to change without notice. The author and publisher of this book reserve the right to make changes to the content of this book at any time and without notice.

By reading this book, you agree that the author and publisher of this book are not responsible for any losses incurred from Forex trading. You also acknowledge that you are solely responsible for any investment or financial decisions you make based on the information contained in this book.

In conclusion, the information contained in this book is for educational purposes only, and the author and publisher of this book are not responsible for any losses incurred from Forex trading. You should always seek professional financial or investment advice before making any investment or financial decisions.

Table Of Content

Introduction

Welcome to the exciting and at times perplexing world of Forex trading! Have you ever wondered what it takes to trade the financial markets or heard the term Forex thrown around at a dinner party and thought it was a type of exotic food?

Well, this book is designed to guide you through the basics – advanced knowledge of currency trading, and help you get started on your journey to becoming a successful trader.

Now, you might be thinking, "Isn't Forex trading only for people with fancy suits and a whole lot of money?" Well, not exactly. In fact, Forex trading is open to anyone with an internet connection and a willingness to learn. But before you dive headfirst into the world of currency trading, it's important to understand what you're getting into.

In this book, we will take a deep dive into Forex trading and cover everything from the basics of currency trading to developing your own trading strategy. We'll explore the different types of trading styles and provide tips and tricks for traders of all levels, from complete beginners to seasoned professionals.

But hold on a second, Janie, "I'm not sure I'm ready for all of this. It sounds confusing and overwhelming."

Don't worry, we'll take it one step at a time and break down the concepts into bite-sized pieces that even your grandma could understand (well, maybe not your grandma, but you get the point).

So, sit back, relax, and get ready to embark on a journey that will not only help you understand the ins and outs of Forex trading but also give you the confidence to start trading on your own. And who knows, maybe you'll even make a fortune along the way (or at least enough to pay for that fancy suit you've been eyeing).

Chapter 1

Introduction to Forex Trading

Forex trading, also known as foreign exchange trading, is the buying and selling of currencies with the goal of making a profit. It is a decentralized market that operates 24 hours a day, five days a week, and is one of the largest financial markets in the world.

Understanding the Forex Market

The Forex market is unique in many ways. Unlike the stock market, which has a central exchange, Forex is a decentralized market, meaning that trading takes place over the counter (OTC) and is conducted electronically between traders around the world. This means that there is no single exchange or clearinghouse, and transactions are conducted directly between buyers and sellers.

Another unique aspect of the Forex market is its size. According to the Bank for International Settlements, the daily turnover in the Forex market is over $6 trillion, making it one of the largest financial markets in the world. This means that there is a lot of liquidity in the market, which can make it easier to enter and exit trades quickly.

Advantages and Disadvantages of Forex Trading

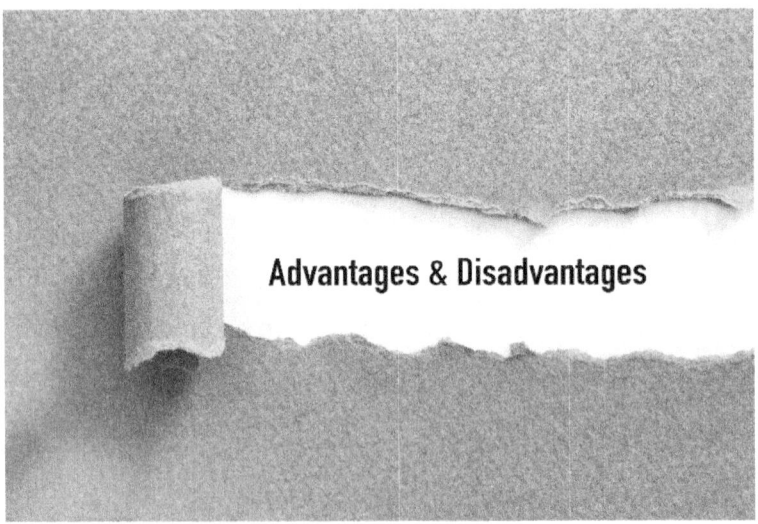

Advantages & Disadvantages

There are several advantages to Forex trading. For one, it is a highly accessible market, with low barriers to entry. You can start trading with as little as a few hundred dollars, and many brokers offer demo accounts that allow you to practice trading without risking any real money.

Another advantage of Forex trading is the ability to trade 24 hours a day, five days a week. This means that you can trade whenever it's convenient for you, regardless of your location or time zone. In addition, the Forex market is highly liquid, meaning that you can buy and sell currencies quickly and easily.

However, there are also some disadvantages to Forex trading. One of the biggest is the high degree of volatility in the market. Currencies can fluctuate in value rapidly, and there is always the potential for significant losses if you're not careful.

In addition, Forex trading requires a certain level of knowledge and skill.

While it is possible to make money in the market with little experience, it's important to have a solid understanding of the fundamentals and technical analysis in order to make informed trading decisions.

Forex trading can be a highly rewarding and exciting activity for those who are willing to put in the time and effort to learn the ins and outs of the market.

When you understand the basics of Forex trading, including the mechanics of the market and the advantages and disadvantages of trading, you'll be well on your way to developing your own successful trading strategy.

What Is a Forex Broker

A broker serves as a vital link between traders and the global currency market, providing access to trade various currency pairs.

So, what is a Forex Broker? In simple terms, a forex broker is an intermediary or a middleman between individual traders and the foreign exchange market. They act as a facilitator, enabling traders to buy and sell currencies in the forex market.

Brokers provide the necessary trading platforms, tools, and services that empower traders to execute trades efficiently.

The Role of a Forex Broker

1. Market Access and Liquidity: One of the primary functions of a forex broker is to provide traders with access to the forex market. The broker establishes connections with liquidity providers, such as banks, financial institutions, and other market participants, to ensure there is a continuous flow of liquidity. This ensures that traders can enter and exit trades at any time, even during volatile market conditions.

2. Trading Platforms: Forex brokers offer trading platforms that allow traders to analyze market trends, monitor currency prices, and execute trades. These platforms come equipped with various features like real-time charts, technical analysis tools, and order execution capabilities. Brokers strive to offer user-friendly and feature-rich platforms to enhance the trading experience for their clients.

3. Order Execution: Efficient order execution is crucial in forex trading, and brokers play a significant role in this process. When traders place their orders, brokers execute them on their behalf, striving to achieve the best possible prices. They provide different order types, such as market orders, limit orders, and stop orders, giving traders flexibility in managing their trades.

4. Leverage and Margin Trading: Forex brokers often provide traders with leverage, allowing them to control larger positions in the market with a smaller amount of capital. This feature, known as margin trading, can magnify profits but also increases the risk. Brokers ensure that traders understand the implications of leverage and provide risk management tools to help them make informed decisions.

5. Educational Resources and Support: To assist traders in improving their knowledge and skills, forex brokers often offer educational resources, tutorials, webinars, and market analysis. They understand that educated traders are more

likely to make informed decisions and be successful in their trading endeavors. Additionally, brokers provide customer support services to address any queries or technical difficulties faced by their clients.

Let's be honest, Forex brokers play a crucial role in the currency trading space. They provide traders with the necessary tools, platforms, and services to access the Forex market and execute trades efficiently.

They act as intermediaries, brokers ensure liquidity, offer diverse trading options, and contribute to the overall growth and development of the forex trading community.

Remember, when choosing a Forex broker, it's essential to consider factors such as **regulation**, **reputation**, **trading conditions**, and **the quality of their services**. Selecting a reliable and reputable broker sets the foundation for a rewarding trading experience.

Disclaimer: Forex trading involves significant risks, and it's important to conduct thorough research, seek professional advice, and only invest funds you can afford to lose.

Chapter 2

Currency Pairs and Common Forex Terminologies

Understanding currency pairs is essential for any aspiring trader. Currency pairs represent the relative value of one currency against another and are the building blocks of Forex trading.

Well, let's get into the intricacies of currency pairs and explore common Forex terminologies that every trader should be familiar with.

The Structure of Currency Pairs

Currency pairs lie at the heart of forex trading, so it's essential to grasp their structure and significance. A currency pair is a representation of the exchange rate between two distinct currencies.

Trading in the forex market involves buying one currency while simultaneously selling another. Profiting from the fluctuating values of these currencies is the primary goal of forex traders.

Let's explore the currency pair more closely. Take, for example, the US Dollar (USD) and the Euro (EUR). These two currencies form the currency pair EUR/USD. In this pair, the first currency, the Euro (EUR), is referred to as the base currency, and the second, the US Dollar (USD), is the quote currency. The exchange rate between these two currencies reveals the amount of the quote currency needed to purchase one unit of the base currency.

If the EUR/USD exchange rate is 1.2000, this indicates that you need 1.20 US Dollars to acquire one Euro. When you anticipate the base currency to appreciate against the quote currency, you opt to go long or buy the currency pair. On the other hand, if you expect the base currency to depreciate, you go short or sell the currency pair.

Currency Pairs in Forex Trading

As a forex trader, you must have a solid understanding of currency pairs. This knowledge empowers you to navigate the world of forex trading with ease and success.

Currency pairs hold the key to unlocking profits. These pairs represent the exchange rate between two currencies, and they play a pivotal role in determining the profitability of your trades. At its core, forex trading is all about buying one currency and selling another simultaneously.

This is where currency pairs come into play, as they offer a standardized way to trade currencies.

Now, you might wonder, what exactly are these currency pairs? Imagine you're at the airport and need to exchange your US dollars for Euros. The exchange rate you see displayed is, in fact, a currency pair.

In forex trading, currency pairs are denoted by a three-letter code for each currency involved. For example, the currency pair for US dollars and Euros would be written as USD/EUR.

An interesting aspect of currency pairs is the 'base' and 'quote' currency distinction. The base currency is the first currency in the pair, while the quote currency is the second one. The exchange rate between the two currencies signifies how much of the quote currency you would need to buy one unit of the base currency.

For instance, if the USD/EUR exchange rate is 0.85, it means you would require 0.85 Euros to purchase one US dollar. So, when you're trading currency pairs, it's vital to keep an eye on the exchange rate fluctuations, as they directly impact on your bottom line.

Different currency pairs exhibit distinct characteristics, such as volatility, popularity, and trading volume. By familiarizing yourself with these factors, you can make more informed decisions and tailor your trading strategies accordingly.

Types of Currency Pairs, Popularity, Volatility, and Liquidity

Currency pairs can be broadly classified into three categories: major pairs, minor pairs, and exotic pairs.

MAJOR PAIRS

Major currency pairs consist of the world's most widely traded currencies and have the US dollar (USD) as one of the constituents. These pairs are popular among traders due to their high liquidity, tight spreads, and lower trading costs.

The major currency pairs include:

EUR/USD (Euro/US Dollar)

GBP/USD (British Pound/US Dollar)

USD/JPY (US Dollar/Japanese Yen)

USD/CHF (US Dollar/Swiss Franc)

USD/CAD (US Dollar/Canadian Dollar)

AUD/USD (Australian Dollar/US Dollar)

NZD/USD (New Zealand Dollar/US Dollar)

Generally, major currency pairs exhibit lower volatility compared to minor and exotic pairs. But keep in mind that certain events or economic releases can cause temporary spikes in volatility. Among the major pairs, EUR/USD and GBP/USD tend to be more volatile due to their larger trading volumes and economic ties to global events.

MINOR PAIRS (CROSS CURRENCY PAIRS)

Minor pairs, also known as cross currency pairs, do not include the US dollar. They are typically derived from the major currencies and are less liquid than major pairs.

Some of the widely traded minor currency pairs are:

EUR/GBP (Euro/British Pound)

EUR/CHF (Euro/Swiss Franc)

EUR/JPY (Euro/Japanese Yen)

GBP/CAD (British Pound/Canadian Dollar)

GBP/JPY (British Pound/Japanese Yen)

AUD/JPY (Australian Dollar/Japanese Yen)

CAD/JPY (Canadian Dollar/Japanese Yen)

These pairs tend to have wider spreads and can be more volatile than major pairs, especially during periods of economic uncertainty or global events that impact the involved currencies.

EXOTIC PAIRS

Exotic currency pairs consist of one major currency and one currency from an emerging or smaller economy. Due to their low trading volumes and limited market participants, exotic pairs often have wider spreads and higher trading costs.

Examples of exotic currency pairs include:

USD/SEK (US Dollar/Swedish Krona)

USD/NOK (US Dollar/Norwegian Krone)

USD/ZAR (US Dollar/South African Rand)

USD/SGD (US Dollar/Singapore Dollar)

USD/HKD (US Dollar/Hong Kong Dollar)

Exotic pairs are typically more volatile than major and minor pairs, as they are more susceptible to economic and political events in their respective countries.

Major pairs are the most popular and less volatile, while exotic pairs tend to be the least traded and more volatile. By selecting the appropriate currency pairs based on your trading style and risk appetite, you can optimize your forex trading experience and enhance your profitability.

When it comes to forex trading, the concept of 'pip' is crucial. A pip represents the smallest price movement in a currency pair, and it's typically equal to 0.0001, except for currency pairs involving the Japanese yen. Understanding pips is essential for calculating your potential profits and losses.

Currency pairs are the lifeblood of forex trading. As you progress in your trading, recognizing the types of currency pairs available to you and their inherent characteristics can profoundly influence your success.

Choose the right currency pairs that align with your trading style, risk tolerance, and market knowledge. This will help optimize your trading experience and enhance your profitability.

Forex Terminologies

Pip: A pip stands for "percentage in point" and is the smallest unit of measurement in Forex trading. It represents the fourth decimal place in most currency pairs and denotes the price movement.

Bid and Ask Price: The bid price represents the price at which the market is willing to buy the base currency, while the ask price represents the price at which the market is willing to sell the base currency. The difference between the bid and ask price is called the spread.

Spread: The spread refers to the difference between the bid and ask price and represents the cost of trading. It is typically measured in pips and varies across different currency pairs and market conditions.

Long and Short Positions: Going long means buying a currency pair in anticipation of its value increasing. Conversely, going short refers to selling a currency pair with the expectation that its value will decrease. Traders can profit from both rising and falling markets.

Leverage: Leverage allows traders to control larger positions with a smaller amount of capital. It amplifies both profits and losses, so traders must exercise caution when using leverage.

Stop-Loss Order: A stop-loss order is a risk management tool used by traders to limit potential losses. It is a predetermined order that automatically closes a trade when the price reaches a specified level.

Fundamental and Technical Analysis: Fundamental analysis involves evaluating the economic, political, and social factors that influence currency values. It provides insight into the long-term direction of a currency pair.

Technical analysis, on the other hand, focuses on historical price data and uses various tools, such as chart patterns and technical indicators, to identify potential trade opportunities and make informed decisions.

Swap or Rollover: A swap, also known as a rollover, is the interest paid or earned for holding a forex position overnight. It is based on the interest rate differential between the two currencies involved in the currency pair. Depending on the direction of your trade and the interest rate difference, you may either receive or pay a swap fee.

Slippage: Slippage is the difference between the expected price of a trade and the price at which the trade is actually executed. It usually occurs during periods of high volatility or low liquidity in the market. Slippage can affect your trading results, so it's essential to be aware of the potential impact and choose a broker with minimal slippage.

Understanding currency pairs and how they move will help you decide which pair and assets best suit your trading style. Some pairs/assets move slower, while others are very volatile.

So, we've learned the fundamental concepts of currency pairs and familiarized ourselves with common Forex terminologies. Next, we'll go through some basic trading tools every beginner trader should know. Shall we?

Chapter 3

Essential Trading Tools for Beginners

Forex trading can be intimidating for beginners, especially if you don't have the right tools to help you navigate the market. In this chapter, we'll discuss some of the essential trading tools you need as a beginner in Forex trading.

Understanding Trading Platforms

A trading platform is software that connects traders to their brokerage accounts, providing them with real-time access to the Forex market. Understanding how a trading platform works is crucial for beginners, as it provides the foundation for executing trades.

There are several trading platforms available, each with unique features and functionalities.

One of the most popular trading platforms is MetaTrader 4 (MT4), which is widely used by Forex traders around the world. MT4 provides traders with access to live streaming quotes, real-time charting, and a wide range of analytical tools that can help traders make informed trading decisions. Other popular trading platforms include cTrader, NinjaTrader, and TradingView.

Types of Trading Charts and Indicators

Trading charts are graphical representations of the price movements of currency pairs over time. They are used to identify patterns and trends in the market, helping traders make informed trading decisions. There are several types of trading charts available, including line charts, bar charts, and candlestick charts.

Candlestick charts are the most used charts in Forex trading due to their ease of use and their ability to provide detailed information about price movements. They are made up of candlestick patterns, each representing a specific time period, such as a minute, hour, or day.

To see step by step how to be MT4 ready, check out my tutorial here:

https://www.youtube.com/watch?v=ZIDPfMfXJk4

In addition to trading charts, indicators are also essential tools for Forex traders. Indicators are mathematical calculations that are plotted on a trading chart, providing additional information about price movements. They are used to identify trends, reversals, and other key market conditions.

Some of the most popular indicators in Forex trading include Moving averages, Relative Strength Index (RSI), and Bollinger Bands, and MACD. Traders can use these indicators to help them identify potential entry and exit points, as well as to confirm trends and price movements.

Setting up a Trading Account

To start trading Forex, you need to set up a trading account with a Forex broker. Choosing a broker can be overwhelming, as there are many options available. When selecting a broker, you should consider factors such as regulation, fees, and trading platforms.

Once you have selected a broker, you will need to set up your trading account. This typically involves filling out an online application and providing identification and other personal information. You will also need to fund your account with an initial deposit, which can vary depending on the broker.

Before funding your account, you should also consider the different payment methods available, such as bank transfers, credit cards, or e-wallets. Each payment method has different processing times and fees, so it's important to choose one that works best for you.

So, take the time to explore these different trading platforms, study and experiment the trading charts and indicators you find on these platforms, and setup a trading account.

5 Most Common Trading Indicators

Moving averages: are a popular statistical tool used to analyze trends in time series data. The basic idea behind a moving average is to smooth out fluctuations in the data by averaging out values over a certain period of time, such as the last 10 days or the last month.

This can help reveal underlying trends in the data and make it easier to spot patterns and changes over time. Moving averages can be simple, weighted, or exponential, depending on the weighting given to each data point in the calculation.

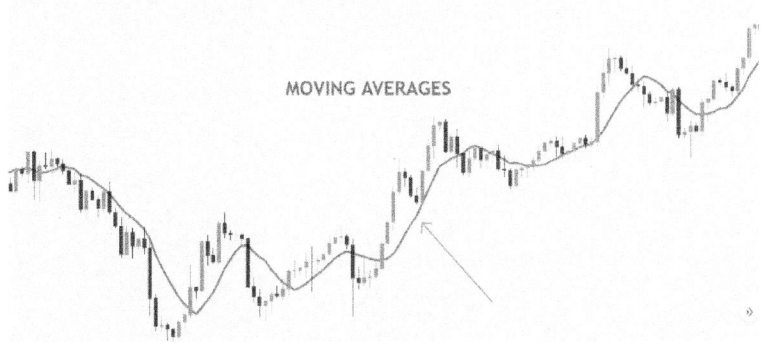

MOVING AVERAGES

Overall, moving averages are a useful and versatile tool for anyone interested in analyzing time series data.

VWAP: stands for Volume-Weighted Average Price, and it is a popular trading indicator used by many traders and investors. The VWAP is calculated by taking the average price of a security over a specified time period, weighted by the volume traded at each price level.

The VWAP is often used as a benchmark to evaluate whether a trade was executed at a fair price, as it takes into account both price and volume. Traders often use the VWAP to help determine the best times to buy or sell a security, as prices above the VWAP are generally considered bullish, while prices below the VWAP are generally considered bearish.

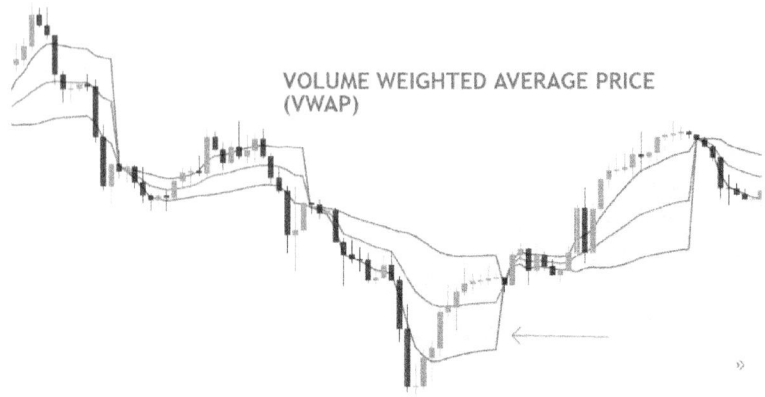

VOLUME WEIGHTED AVERAGE PRICE (VWAP)

Overall, the VWAP is a useful tool for traders looking to gain insights into market trends and make more informed trading decisions.

RSI: stands for Relative Strength Index, and it is a momentum oscillator that is commonly used in technical analysis to measure the strength of a security's price action. The RSI is calculated by comparing the average gains and losses of a security over a specified time period, typically 14 days.

The resulting value ranges from 0 to 100, with values above 70 indicating overbought conditions, and values below 30 indicating oversold conditions.

RELETIVE STRENGTH INDEX (RSI)

Traders often use the RSI to identify potential trend reversals and to confirm the strength of existing trends.

The RSI is a popular and versatile tool in technical analysis that can be applied to a wide variety of securities and time frames.

MACD: stands for Moving Average Convergence Divergence, and it is a trend-following momentum indicator used in technical analysis to identify changes in the strength, direction, and duration of a security's price trend.

The MACD is calculated by subtracting a longer-term exponential moving average (EMA) from a shorter-term EMA and plotting the difference as a histogram. A signal line, which is usually a 9-period EMA of the MACD, is then plotted on top of the histogram to generate buy and sell signals.

MOVING AVERAGE CONVERGENCE DIVERGENCE (MACD)

Traders often use the MACD to identify bullish and bearish momentum, and to confirm the strength of existing trends.

The MACD is a popular and widely used tool in technical analysis, particularly in the analysis of stock and Forex markets.

Chapter 4

Mastering Candlesticks

Candlesticks are the building blocks of forex trading charts, providing invaluable insights into price movements. Each candlestick represents a specific time period and consists of four essential elements: the opening price, closing price, highest price, and lowest price within that period.

The good thing about understanding and interpreting candlesticks is that you will not only gain a deeper understanding of market sentiment, but also be able to make better predictions.

Basic Candlestick Patterns

The Doji:

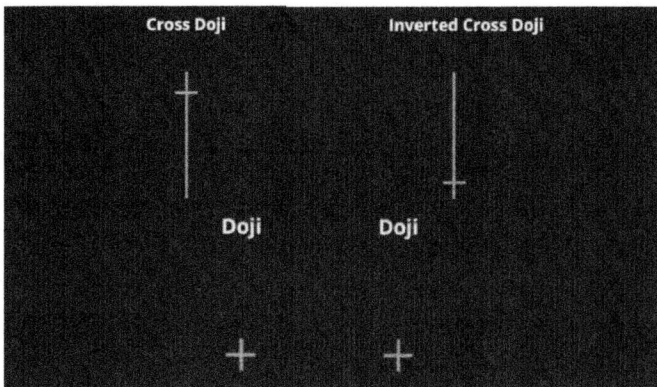

This peculiar candlestick has a small body with a nearly equal opening and closing price. It signifies market indecision and suggests a potential reversal in the trend.

The Hammer and Shooting Star:

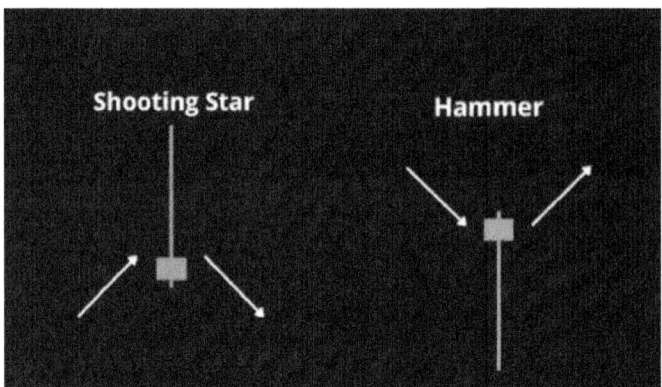

The hammer resembles an actual hammer, and this bullish candlestick has a small body with a long lower wick. It indicates a potential bullish reversal after a downtrend, signaling buying pressure.

The shooting star has a small body with a long upper wick and a small or nonexistent lower wick. This bearish candlestick suggests a potential reversal from an uptrend, indicating selling pressure.

The Engulfing Pattern:

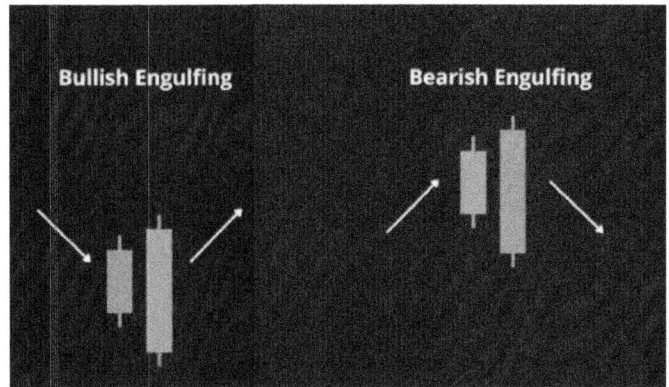

These patterns occurs when one candlestick engulfs the body of the previous candlestick. A bullish engulfing pattern signals a potential uptrend reversal, while a bearish engulfing pattern indicates a potential downtrend reversal.

Advanced Candlestick Patterns

The Morning and Evening Star:

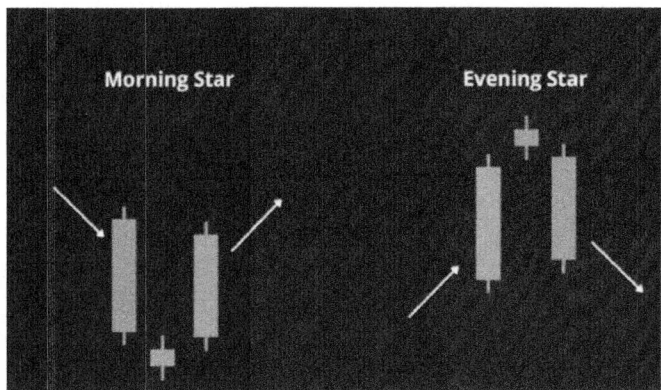

The Evening Star appears at the end of an uptrend, consisting of three candlesticks.

The first candlestick is a bullish candle, representing the prevailing uptrend. The second candlestick is a small-bodied or doji candle that indicates market indecision or a weakening of bullish momentum. The third candlestick is a bearish candle that closes below the midpoint of the first candle, suggesting increased selling pressure and a potential trend reversal.

The Morning Star pattern is the bullish counterpart of the Evening Star. It forms at the end of a downtrend and suggests a potential trend reversal to the upside. Similar to the Evening Star, it also consists of three candlesticks.

The first candlestick is a bearish candle, representing the prevailing downtrend. The second candlestick is a small-bodied or doji candle that indicates market indecision or a weakening of bearish momentum. The third candlestick is a bullish candle that closes above the midpoint of the first candle, signaling increased buying pressure and a potential trend reversal.

The Bullish and Bearish Harami:
The bullish harami consists of two candlesticks, with the first being a long bearish candlestick and the second a small-bodied bullish candlestick. It suggests a potential bullish reversal.

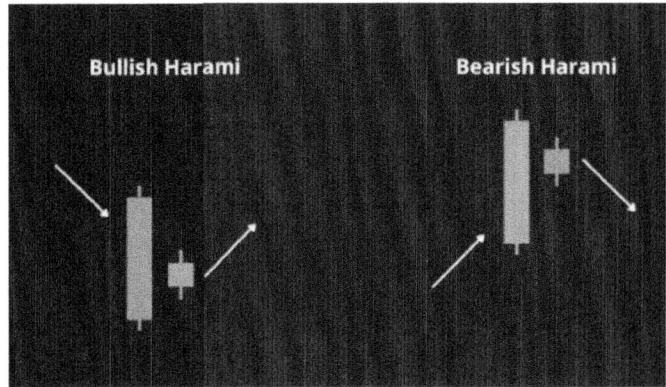

Similar to the bullish harami, this pattern consists of a long bullish candlestick followed by a small-bodied bearish candlestick. It indicates a potential bearish reversal.

The Three White Soldiers:

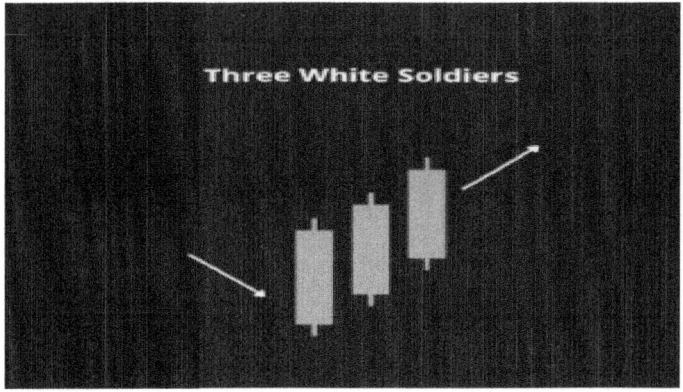

The Three White Soldiers pattern is a bullish reversal formation that consists of three consecutive bullish candlesticks. It typically occurs after a downtrend and signals a potential trend reversal to the upside.

Each candlestick in the pattern is a long bullish candle with little to no upper wicks, indicating strong buying pressure. Each subsequent candlestick opens within the body of the previous candle and closes higher, reflecting increasing bullish momentum.

The Three White Soldiers pattern suggests a strong shift in market sentiment from bearish to bullish, indicating a potential uptrend.

The Three Black Crows:

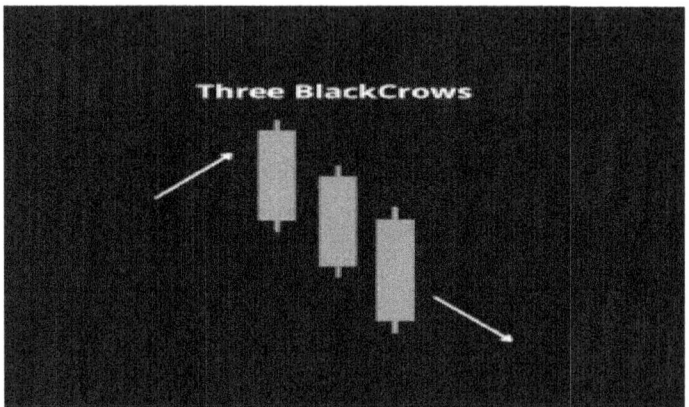

The Three Black Crows pattern is the bearish counterpart of the Three White Soldiers pattern. It occurs after an uptrend and signals a potential trend reversal to the downside.

Each candlestick in the pattern is a long bearish candle with little to no lower wicks, indicating strong selling pressure. Each subsequent candlestick opens within the body of the previous candle and closes lower, reflecting increasing bearish momentum.

The Three Black Crows pattern suggests a strong shift in market sentiment from bullish to bearish, indicating a potential downtrend.

The Rising Three Methods:

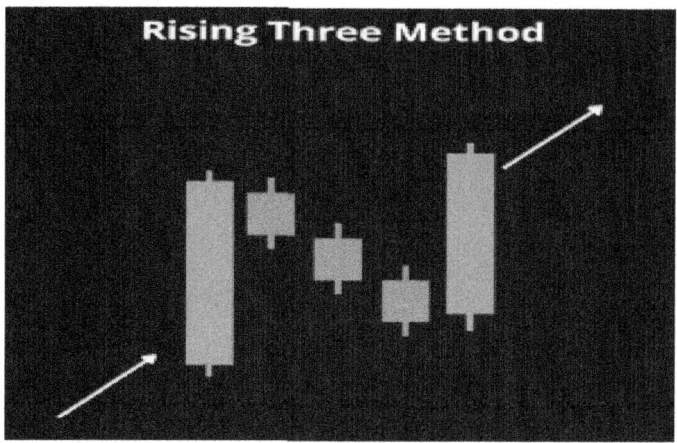

The Rising Three Methods is a bullish continuation pattern that forms during an uptrend. It indicates a temporary pause in the upward movement before the prevailing trend resumes.

 The first candlestick is a long bullish candle that represents the established uptrend.
The next three candlesticks are smaller-bodied bearish candles that trade within the high and low range of the first candlestick, indicating a consolidation or sideways movement.

The fifth candlestick is a long bullish candle that breaks out of the consolidation, confirming the continuation of the uptrend. The Rising Three Methods pattern suggests that buyers are taking a breather but are still in control, hinting at the resumption of the upward movement.

Interpreting Candlestick Patterns

To truly master candlesticks and unlock their full potential, you'll need to combine pattern recognition with other technical indicators and analysis tools. When you incorporate additional factors into your analysis, you can enhance the accuracy of your predictions.

Here are some key elements to consider when interpreting candlestick patterns:

Volume:
Volume is a crucial factor in candlestick analysis as it provides insight into the strength behind price movements. When analyzing candlestick patterns, it is important to pay attention to volume levels.

High volume during a specific candlestick pattern suggests strong market participation and validates the significance of the pattern. Conversely, low volume may indicate a lack of conviction and decrease the reliability of the pattern. By considering volume alongside candlestick patterns, you can better gauge the reliability of potential market reversals or continuations.

Trendlines:
Trendlines are invaluable tools that help identify the prevailing direction of a market trend. When analyzing candlestick patterns, it is crucial to assess how they interact with trendlines. An established trendline can provide confirmation or contradiction to the candlestick pattern's interpretation.

For instance, a bullish candlestick pattern that occurs near an upward trendline reinforces the potential for a bullish continuation. Conversely, a bearish candlestick pattern near a downward trendline strengthens the likelihood of a bearish continuation.

When you integrate trendlines with candlestick analysis, you can gain a comprehensive view of market dynamics.

Support and Resistance Levels:
Support and resistance levels are significant price levels where buying or selling pressure is expected to be strong.

When analyzing candlestick patterns, it is essential to consider their proximity to key support and resistance levels.

A candlestick pattern that forms near a strong support level increases the likelihood of a bullish reversal. Conversely, a candlestick pattern forming near a resistance level suggests a higher probability of a bearish reversal.

Including support and resistance levels into your analysis helps validate the reliability of candlestick patterns and provides crucial context for decision-making.

Moving Averages:
Moving averages smooth out price data and help identify the underlying trend. When combined with candlestick analysis, moving averages provide valuable confirmation signals.

For example, if a bullish candlestick pattern occurs above a rising 50-day moving average, it strengthens the potential for a bullish continuation. Conversely, a bearish candlestick pattern below a declining 200-day moving average reinforces the likelihood of a bearish continuation.

So, what I'm I saying? Incorporating these additional factors into your candlestick analysis, can enhance your ability to predict future price movements with greater accuracy.

Just remember that mastering candlestick patterns requires continuous learning and practice. Over time, with diligent observation and analysis, you will develop the skills to interpret candlestick patterns more effectively.

Putting Candlestick Analysis into Action

Here are the steps you should follow.

Study Historical Charts:

To apply your knowledge of candlestick analysis effectively, start by immersing yourself in historical price charts. Observe different timeframes, from short-term to long-term, and analyze how candlestick patterns have influenced price movements in the past.

Take note of recurring patterns and their outcomes, paying attention to the context in which they appear. Studying historical charts will help you develop an intuition for recognizing candlestick patterns in real-time trading situations.

Identify Various Candlestick Patterns:

As you delve into historical charts, familiarize yourself with a wide range of candlestick patterns. Expand beyond the basic patterns mentioned earlier and explore more complex formations, such as the hanging man, engulfing patterns with multiple candles, and the morning star.

Each pattern carries its own significance and provides unique insights into market sentiment. Make it a habit to identify these patterns accurately and understand their potential implications for future price movements.

Practice on Demo Accounts:

To gain hands-on experience and refine your skills, utilize demo accounts offered by forex trading platforms. These accounts provide a risk-free environment where you can apply your candlestick analysis techniques in real-time trading scenarios.

Execute trades based on the patterns you identify and assess the outcomes. You should use this opportunity to fine-tune your entry and exit strategies, validate the effectiveness of your analysis, and build your confidence.

Gradually Transition to Real Trading:

Once you've gained proficiency in candlestick analysis through practice on demo accounts, it's time to transition to real trading. However, it's crucial to approach this transition gradually and cautiously.

Start with small trading positions and limit your exposure until you feel comfortable executing trades based on candlestick patterns in a live trading environment. Real trading involves real risks, and emotions can come into play, so it's important to maintain discipline and adhere to your trading plan.

Prioritize Risk Management:

Throughout your trading journey, from demo accounts to real trading, always prioritize risk management. Candlestick analysis is a great tool, but it is not without flaws. Implement appropriate stop-loss orders and risk-reward ratios to protect your capital.

Set realistic profit targets and don't succumb to the temptation of chasing trades solely based on candlestick patterns. Remember that risk management is an integral part of successful trading, and it will safeguard you against potential losses.

Continually to refine your skills, adapt to changing market conditions, and stay open to learning and evolving as a trader. With a solid foundation in candlestick analysis and a disciplined approach, you'll be well-equipped to make informed trading decisions and capitalize on the opportunities presented by the forex market.

Mastering candlesticks is like learning a new language in a foreign country. You'll understand what the people are saying. In Forex, you'll better interpret the charts.

Chapter 5

Fundamental Analysis for Forex Trading

Fundamental analysis is a method of analyzing financial markets by examining macroeconomic and geopolitical events, as well as the financial statements of companies, to determine the value of an asset. It is a crucial aspect of Forex trading, as it helps traders to understand the underlying factors that influence the currency market.

What is Fundamental Analysis?

Fundamental analysis in Forex trading involves analyzing various economic and political factors that can affect the value of a currency.

These factors include interest rates, inflation rates, gross domestic product (GDP), employment data, and trade balance. Traders who use fundamental analysis believe that these factors can help predict future currency movements.

Economic Indicators that Affect the Forex Market

One of the key components of fundamental analysis is economic indicators. Economic indicators are statistical measures that reflect the performance of an economy. They provide information on the health of an economy and its potential for growth or contraction. Some of the most important economic indicators that traders follow in Forex trading include:

Gross Domestic Product (GDP) - The Gross Domestic Product (GDP) is one of the most important economic indicators, and traders all over the world keep a constant eye on it.

GDP is the total worth of all products and services produced in a country over a specific time period, usually a quarter or a year. It is regarded as a measure of economic strength because a greater GDP usually signifies a healthy and expanding economy.

GDP statistics can be susceptible to adjustments, making it difficult to comprehend and trade on in the short term. Furthermore, the impact of GDP on the currency market can be influenced by a number of factors, including market expectations, the overall status of the economy, and the mix of GDP growth.

For example, if a country's GDP growth is predominantly driven by consumer spending, this can indicate economic health and potentially lead to a stronger currency.

On the other hand, if a country's GDP growth is predominantly driven by government expenditure, this might raise inflationary fears and perhaps lead to a weaker currency.

CPI and PPI – The Producer Price Index (PPI) and Consumer Price Index (CPI) are two of the most closely monitored economic indicators for Forex traders since they provide insight into the economy's inflationary tendencies.

The Producer Price Index (PPI) tracks price changes at the producer level, before products and services are supplied to consumers. Everything from raw ingredients to completed goods might be included.

PPI changes can indicate trends in inflationary pressures, as increased producer prices can eventually lead to higher consumer prices.

The CPI, on the other hand, measures changes in consumer prices. Everything from food and clothing to shelter and healthcare is included. Changes in the Consumer Price Index (CPI) can provide information on the cost of living for consumers as well as changes in inflationary pressures.

As a Forex trader, it's critical to monitor both the PPI and the CPI, because fluctuations in inflation can have a major impact on currency values.

Inflation can cause interest rates to rise, making a currency more appealing to investors.

However, if inflation becomes too high, it might cause the currency to weaken as investors become concerned about the economy's solidity.

Interest Rates – Interest rates set by central banks can have a significant impact on a currency's value. A higher interest rate can make a currency more attractive to foreign investors, leading to an increase in its value.

Employment Data – The employment data of a country can provide insights into the health of its economy. Strong employment data can indicate a growing economy, which can lead to an increase in the value of its currency.

A greater unemployment rate may suggest a poor economy, whilst a lower rate may indicate a better economy. However, the true impact of the unemployment rate on the FX market depends on a number of factors, including the environment in which the statistic is issued and traders' expectations.

Nonfarm Payrolls (NFP) – These are a widely anticipated monthly economic indicator that gauges the number of employments created or lost in the US economy's nonfarm sector. The US Bureau of Labour Statistics releases this data on the first Friday of each month, and it can have a big impact on the FX market.

The NFP report is an important indicator of the health of the US labour market and provides insight into the economy's overall soundness.

A higher NFP figure signals job growth and possible economic strength, whilst a lower one indicates job losses and potential economic weakness. As a result, the value of the US dollar and other currencies traded against it may suffer.

The NFP report can greatly impact price movement.

For example, if the NFP figure is much higher than predicted, it may indicate increased demand for goods and services as well as an overheating economy, which could lead to greater inflation and higher interest rates.

Retail Sale – Retail sales are an important economic indicator that gauges the total value of products sold by retailers during a specific time period. This data release sheds light on consumer purchasing habits, which are a major driver of economic growth.

A greater retail sales figure may imply a healthy economy and, as a result, higher interest rates, whereas a lower one may indicate weakness.

Changes in consumer spending can have a variety of effects on different sectors of the economy, causing traders to react in a different of ways.

Federal Open Market Committee (FOMC) – This is a significant component of the US Federal Reserve System and is in charge of monetary policy in the US. The FOMC is comprised of 12 members, including seven members of the Federal Reserve System's

Board of Governors and five Reserve Bank presidents.

The FOMC's main objective is to determine the federal funds rate, which is the interest rate at which banks lend to one another overnight. Changes in the federal funds rate can have a big impact on the economy and the Forex market since they affect currency value.

Following each meeting, the FOMC issues a statement that provides insight into the committee's views on the current status of the economy and its future prospects.

This statement can assist traders in determining if trading the Forex markets at that time is a smart idea or not, as it can offer traders with valuable information regarding the direction of monetary policy and anticipated future interest rate changes.

Purchasing Managers' Index (PMI) – PMI assesses the health of the manufacturing sector by measuring changes in output, new orders, and employment.

A higher PMI indicates economic strength, whereas a lower score indicates economic weakness. The PMI is based on a survey of purchasing managers in the manufacturing industry, who are polled on topics such as production levels, new orders, and employment.

The PMI is published monthly and is carefully watched by traders as a measure of economic strength. A value above 50 implies that the manufacturing sector is expanding, while a reading below 50 suggests that it is contracting.

The PMI has the potential to have a significant impact on the FX market.

Chapter 6

Technical Analysis for Forex Trading

Technical analysis, which examines past price and volume data, is a common approach of analyzing the Forex market. It is predicated on the notion that market trends and patterns repeat themselves over time.

Technical analysis is the inverse of fundamental analysis, which uses economic and financial facts to determine a currency's value.

Short-term traders who wish to profit from market price fluctuations frequently utilize technical analysis.

Price Action in Forex trading

Price action in Forex trading refers to the analysis and interpretation of the movement of currency prices on a chart. It is a popular approach among traders who rely on the raw price data rather than using traditional indicators or oscillators.

Price action traders believe that all the necessary information to make trading decisions can be derived from studying the patterns and formations created by price movements.

By closely observing price action, traders aim to identify recurring patterns, such as support and resistance levels, trendlines, chart patterns, and candlestick formations. These patterns provide valuable insights into market sentiment and can help predict future price movements.

Price action analysis involves assessing factors such as the strength of buying or selling pressure, the presence of significant price levels, and the overall market structure.

One of the key advantages of price action trading is its simplicity and ability to adapt to different market conditions.

Traders who employ this approach focus on understanding the dynamics between buyers and sellers, rather than relying on complex indicators or algorithms.

This allows them to develop a deeper understanding of market behavior and make more informed trading decisions.

Price action trading also emphasizes risk management and trade discipline. Traders using this methodology often employ techniques like setting proper stop-loss orders and monitoring price levels that invalidate their trading setups.

By having a clear understanding of potential risks and rewards, price action traders aim to achieve consistent profitability in the Forex market.

So, price action in Forex trading is a strategy that involves analyzing and interpreting the movement of currency prices on a chart. It relies on studying patterns, formations, and market structure to make informed trading decisions.

When you focus on raw price data, price action traders aim to gain insights into market sentiment and predict future price movements, while also prioritizing risk management and trade discipline.

Trading Charts and Their Applications

The image below shows a list of different charts you can use on Tradingview.

You also have various options available to you on other trading platforms so feel free to experiment and show which one suits your trading style better.

Line charts, bar charts, and candlestick charts are the three basic types of charts used in technical analysis.

Line charts - are the most basic sort of chart, and they are made by graphing the closing price of a currency pair over a given time period.

I'▼ TradingView

They are useful for identifying long-term market patterns.

Bar charts - are simpler but contain more information than line charts. They show a currency pair's opening, high, low, and closing prices for a given time period.
Each bar on the graph indicates a different time period, such as a day, week, or month. Bar charts can assist traders notice short-term price movements and make trading decisions based on these movements.

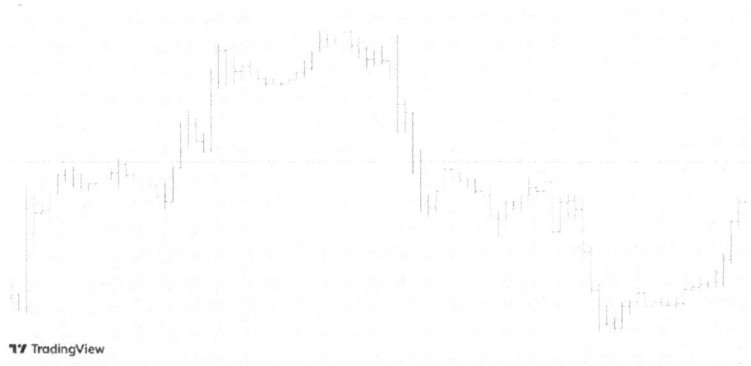

Candlestick charts - are similar to bar charts in appearance but contain more information. They show the same data as bar charts, but they utilize different colors and shapes to illustrate price fluctuations.

A green candlestick, for example, represents a bullish candle, indicating that the closing price is greater than the opening price. A black candlestick, on the other hand, signifies a bearish candle, indicating that the closing price is lower than the opening price.

Keep in mind that you can change the colors of your candle stick to whatever colors you prefer in the setting of your trading platform.

Candlestick charts are excellent for recognising market trends and patterns and can assist traders in making trading decisions based on these patterns.

Candlestick dates back to early Japan, are what most retail traders use to analyze the Forex market. Traders also use candlestick charts to often determine possible price movement based on past patterns.

As a trader the candlesticks are useful when trading as they show the four major price points (open, close, high, and low) throughout the period the trader specifies either H1 H4 or daily charts.

Identifying Trends and Chart Patterns

One of the main importance of technical analysis is to discover **market trends** and **patterns**. The direction of price movement in the market is referred to as a trend. Trends are classified into three types: uptrends, downtrends, and sideways trends.

Market Trends

An uptrend is defined by a succession of higher highs and higher lows, reflecting an optimistic market mood. During an upswing, a trader may hunt for opportunities to buy because the price is likely to rise further.

A **downtrend** is the inverse of an uptrend, characterized by a succession of lower highs and lower lows that indicate a bearish attitude. During a downtrend, traders may hunt for opportunities to sell because the price is projected to fall further.

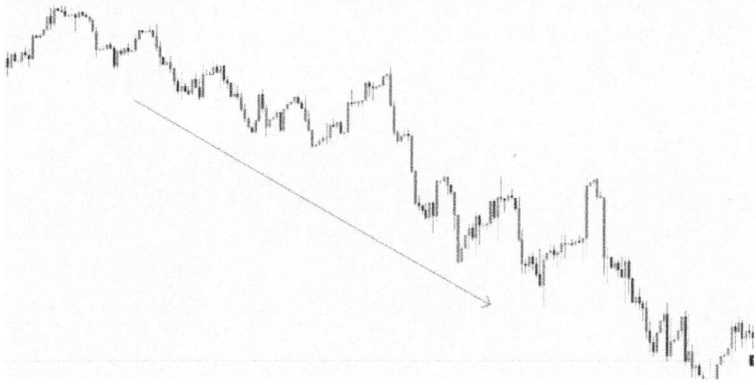

A sideways trend, also known as a ranging market, is characterized by price movements within a relatively narrow range. It is defined by a lack of distinct market direction, with prices moving within a specified range.

Traders may look for opportunities to buy at the lower end of the range and sell at the upper end, although this requires careful analysis to avoid getting caught in false breakouts.

Traders who love to scalp the market, tend to trade during a sideways market trend. But a lot of experience in needed other wise you might get stuck in the middle.

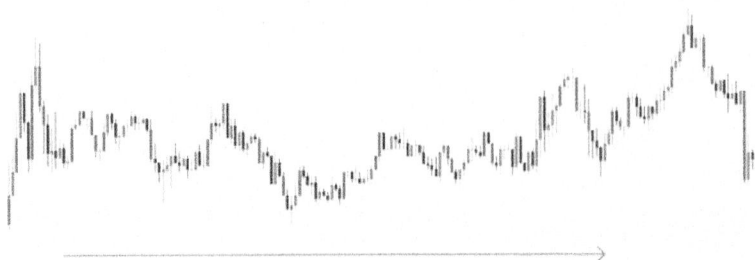

Chart Patterns

Forex trading involves analyzing and interpreting vast amounts of financial data to make better decisions about buying or selling currencies. One of the most effective ways to do this is by using chart patterns.

Chart patterns refer to distinct market formations that can provide insight into future price movements.
These patterns are visual representations of price movements on a chart, which traders can use to predict future price movements.

There are various chart patterns in Forex, and each one has its unique characteristics and interpretation. Here are some of the most commonly used chart patterns in Forex trading:

Head and Shoulders Pattern

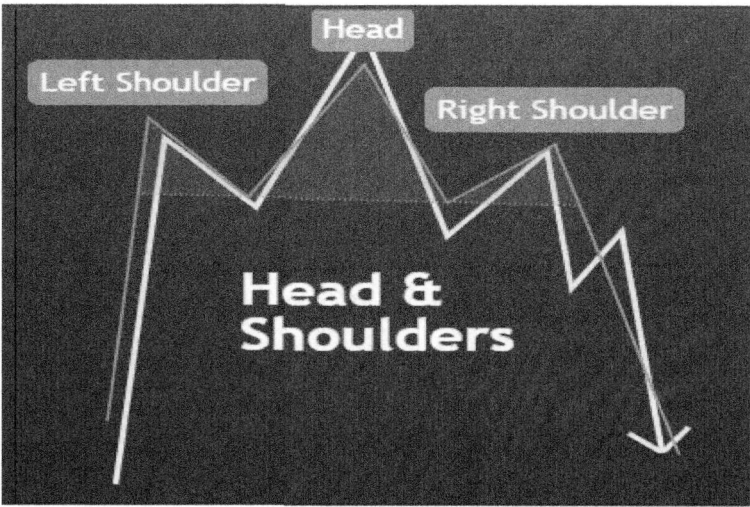

The head and shoulders pattern is a reversal pattern that indicates a possible trend change. It has three summits, the highest of which is in the middle. The two peaks on the sides are known as shoulders, while the centre peak is known as the head.

A bearish reversal occurs when the price breaks below the neckline.

Double Top/Bottom Pattern
A double top/bottom pattern is a reversal pattern that occurs when the price reaches a high/low level twice and fails to break above/below that level. It implies that the trend is losing traction and that a reversal is possible.

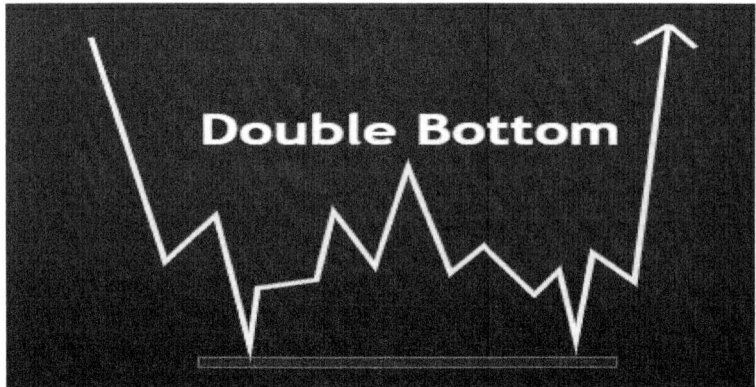

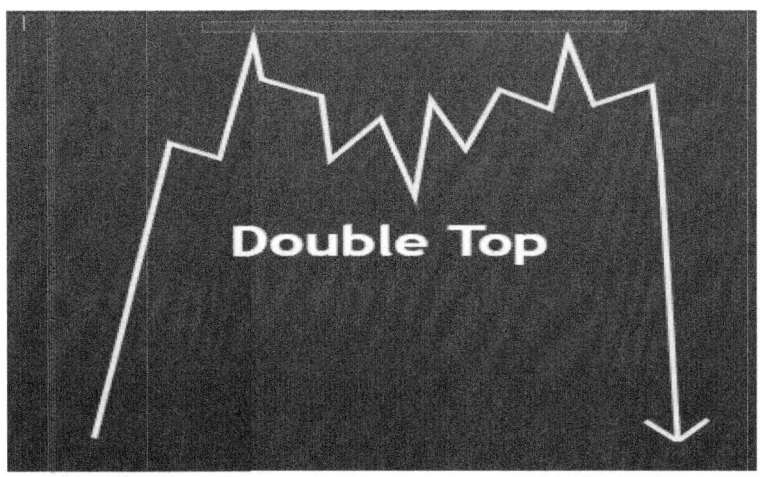

Triangle Pattern

When the price is consolidating within a converging range, the triangle pattern forms as a continuation pattern.

It indicates a period of market hesitation, and traders watch for a breakout in either direction to validate the trend's persistence.

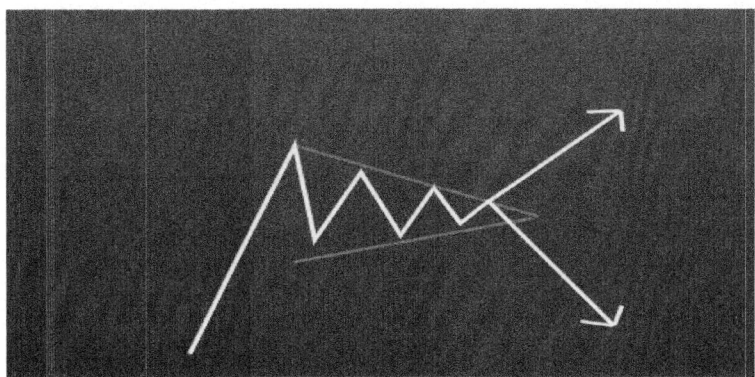

Flag and Pennant Pattern

Flag and pennant patterns are continuation patterns that form following a large price shift.

They are generated by a period of consolidation in which the price moves in a narrow range before breaking out in the opposite direction of the previous trend.

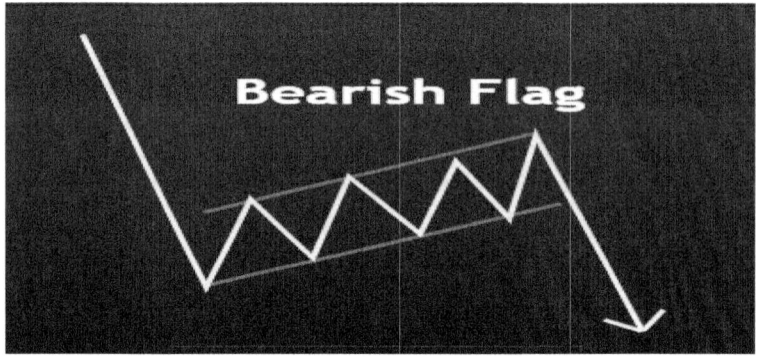

Wedge Pattern

The wedge pattern is a reversal or continuation pattern that appears when price is consolidating inside a converging range, but unlike the triangle pattern, it is inclined in one direction.

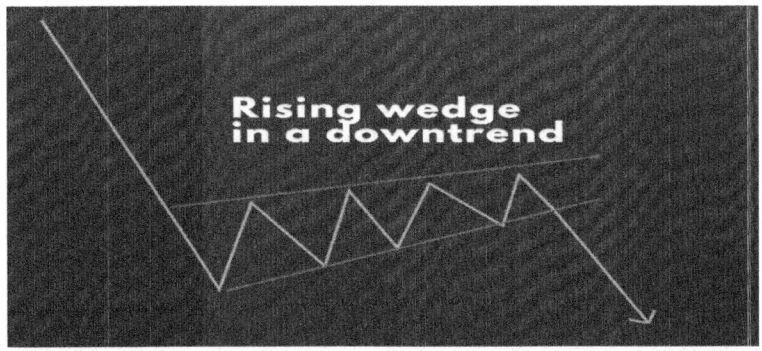

When the price breaks out of the wedge, it suggests a weakening trend and a potential reversal.

So, chart patterns are an important tool for Forex traders because they provide insight into probable price movements and enable better educated decision-making.

However, it is crucial to note that chart patterns are not always 100% accurate, and traders should always support their analysis with other technical indicators and fundamental analysis.

Technical analysis is a key component of Forex trading.
Traders can use technical analysis to discover market trends and patterns, and let me tell you, understanding the many types of charts and how to utilize them, as well as spotting trends and price patterns, are key parts of technical analysis that traders must grasp in order to be successful in Forex trading.

To learn more about how to know when a trend is changing, go here: https://youtu.be/T8h-Px-FKkE.

Chapter 7

Multiple Time Frame Analysis

Time frame refers to the duration or period over which price data is analyzed on a chart. It plays a crucial role in determining trading strategies and decision-making processes.

Exploring Different Time Frames

Forex traders have the flexibility to choose from various time frames, ranging from seconds to years. Each time frame offers a distinct perspective on the market and can influence the trading style adopted.

The three most prevalent time frames are short-term, medium-term, and long-term.

Short-term Time Frames:
Short-term time frames typically range from seconds to minutes, such as the 1-minute, 5-minute, or 15-minute charts. These charts provide traders with rapid and precise information about price movements, making them ideal for scalping or day trading strategies.

Short-term traders focus on capturing small price fluctuations within a limited time frame, aiming for quick profits.

Medium-term Time Frames:

Medium-term time frames usually span from hours to a few days, such as the 1-hour, 4-hour, or daily charts. These charts offer a balanced perspective on price trends and allow traders to identify intermediate-term patterns. Medium-term traders seek to capitalize on broader market moves and trends while avoiding excessive market noise associated with shorter time frames.

Long-term Time Frames:
Long-term time frames include weekly, monthly, and yearly charts, and may extend for weeks to months, or even years. These charts provide a comprehensive view of the market and are favored by position traders and investors.

Long-term traders aim to capture significant market trends, enduring price fluctuations to maximize profit potential over an extended period.

The Impact of Multiple Time Frame Analysis

The choice of time frame significantly influences the analysis and trading strategies employed by Forex traders.
One of the primary advantages of multiple timeframe analysis is its ability to reveal the bigger picture. Forex markets can be highly volatile and subject to short-term fluctuations.

However, by analyzing multiple timeframes simultaneously, traders can identify the overarching trends that may not be evident in shorter time frames alone. This broader perspective helps traders avoid getting caught up in short-term noise and enables them to focus on the larger, more significant market movements.

Also, multiple timeframe analysis assists traders in identifying key support and resistance levels. By observing price action across various timeframes, traders can pinpoint significant price levels that have historically influenced market behavior.

These levels function as reference points for traders to gauge potential entry and exit points, providing a higher probability of successful trades.

Another benefit of multiple timeframe analysis is its ability to enhance risk management strategies. By assessing different timeframes, traders can identify the strength and reliability of certain trends.

This information allows them to adjust their risk exposure, accordingly, ensuring that their positions align with the overall market sentiment and reducing the likelihood of being caught on the wrong side of a sudden market reversal.

Incorporating multiple timeframe analysis into Forex trading strategies also enables traders to fine-tune their timing. You will be able to identify potential price patterns or chart formations that may be forming or nearing completion.

This simple knowledge can help you to anticipate market reversals or breakouts, helping you enter or exit trades with greater precision.

Multiple timeframe analysis is an indispensable tool for Forex traders.

Chapter 8

Risk Management in Forex Trading

Forex trading may be a successful and thrilling business, but it can also be perilous if your risk is not properly managed. Proper risk management is critical for successful trading, and it involves understanding and controlling the risks associated with Forex trading.

In this chapter, we will cover the significance of risk management in Forex trading as well as several fundamental risk management approaches.

The Importance of Risk Management

The process of recognising, measuring, and reducing risks in order to reduce their impact on your trading performance is known as risk management.

Forex trading entails substantial risks, such as market volatility, economic events, and geopolitical events, all of which can produce price changes and unanticipated losses. As a result, risk management is crucial for protecting your capital and preserving your trading account.

You see, the Forex market can be very volatile and unpredictable, so as a wise trader you will need to understand the importance of minimizing the risks associated with trading.

Risk management helps traders to control their emotions and avoid making impulsive decisions that can lead to significant losses. By managing risk, traders can ensure that they do not lose more than they can afford to, and their trading account stays healthy.

One of the primary reasons why risk management is essential is to prevent large losses that can wipe out your trading account. For instance, if you are in a trade where you have used a high level of leverage, you can amplify your profits, but at the same time you have amplified your losses as well.

A single losing trade can lead to significant losses if you do not manage your risk properly. So, please always use risk management techniques to limit your losses and protect your capital.

Setting up Stop Loss and Take Profit Orders

One of the most effective ways to manage risk in Forex trading is to use stop loss and take profit orders. A stop loss order is an order to close a trade at a specific price level if the market moves against you.

It helps you limit your losses and prevent significant drawdowns in your trading account.

A take profit order is an order to close a trade at a specific price level if the market moves in your favor. It helps you lock in your profits and avoid giving back your gains to the market.

Setting up stop loss and taking profit orders is straightforward, and most trading platforms offer these features. You can set the stop loss and take profit levels based on your risk appetite and trading strategy.

For example, a conservative trader may prefer a tight stop loss and a small take profit, whereas a more aggressive trader may prefer a wider stop loss and a bigger take profit. It is essential to use stop loss and take profit orders consistently to manage your risk effectively.

Calculating Position Sizes

Another critical aspect of risk management in Forex trading is calculating your position sizes. Position sizing is the process of determining the appropriate amount of capital to risk per trade based on your trading account size and risk tolerance.

It helps you control your risk exposure and avoid overtrading or undertrading.

To calculate your position size, you should consider your trading account size, the percentage of capital you are willing to risk per trade, and the distance between your entry price and your stop loss level.

There are several position sizing calculators available online that can help you determine the appropriate position size based on your trading parameters. A well know position size calculator can be found here: cashbackforex.com.

In general, you should risk no more than 1-2% of your trading account per trade. For instance, if you have a $10,000 trading account and you risk 2% per trade, your maximum risk per trade would be $200. Therefore, you should adjust your position size accordingly to meet this risk management rule.

So, in a nutshell, managing risk is critical to successful Forex trading, and it involves using various techniques to minimize your losses and protect your capital. Stop loss and take profit orders are essential tools to limit your risk exposure and lock in your profits.

Calculating your position size is also crucial to control your risk exposure and avoid overtrading or undertrading.

Always remember that managing your risk properly, can help you improve your trading performance and achieve consistent profits in Forex trading. Isn't that what most traders want? Consistency!

17 Risk Management Rules

- Before trading live, familiarize yourself with how the Forex market works and the risks involved.

- Before opening a live account, it is recommended that you trade on a demo account for at least four months. This is to get experience and get a feel for things.

- Create and stick to a strong trading strategy.

- Discipline is essential when it comes to using your strategy, as switching between strategies will not accelerate your growth as a trader.

- Do not risk more money than you can afford to lose, and never borrow money to trade.

- Don't be greedy; instead, choose a realistic risk/reward profit/loss ratio. Many profitable traders risk no more than 2% of their capital each open position.

- Change the amount proportionate to the risk involved while deciding on a transaction amount.

- Set unique entry and exit points for your trades ahead of time.

- Limit your use of excessive leverage size. Only trade with assets that you have studied and mastered.

- Set take-profit orders at appropriate and realistic goal points to profit.

- Set stop-loss orders to rapidly close losing trades and conserve money, especially if you are not always monitoring the market.

- When you're winning, employ trailing stops to protect your earnings and winnings.

- Prepare for the worst and hope for the best, which means preparing for the worst-case scenarios and bracing yourself for them.

- Do not overtrade, practice restraint, and take breaks to recharge yourself. This prevents you from trading with your emotions.

- When trading, learn to control your emotions; being extremely happy or depressed will not benefit you.

- Stay up to date with fundamental analysis and high impact news in order to stay on top of any new developments and respond appropriately and adequately.

- Most importantly, stick to your risk management rules at all times, even if you think you've spotted a fantastic opportunity to cash in on.

Chapter 9

Developing a Forex Trading Strategy

An effective Forex trading strategy is critical for any trader seeking long-term profits in the financial markets. A trading strategy is a set of rules and guidelines that a trader follows in order to make trading decisions.

This chapter will go over the fundamental components of a good trading strategy, as well as the process of selecting a trading style, building a strategy, testing, and optimizing it.

Choosing a Trading Style

The first stage in building a trading strategy is to select a trading style that is compatible with your personality, risk tolerance, and lifestyle. In Forex trading, there are three main trading styles: day trading, swing trading, and long-term trading.

Day trading entails opening and closing trades on the same trading day. This approach is appropriate for traders with a high-risk tolerance and the ability to make quick decisions in a fast-paced decision-making situation.

Swing trading entails holding trades for several days to several weeks. This technique is appropriate for traders who want a slower pace of trading and are willing to tolerate some market volatility.

Elements of a Successful Trading Strategy

Regardless of the trading style, there are several key elements that every successful trading strategy should have. These include:

Clear Entry and Exit Rules: Based on technical or fundamental analysis, a trading strategy should have clear rules for entering and quitting transactions. This helps to reduce the influence of emotions on trading decisions.

Risk Management: A trading strategy should have a defined risk management plan, which includes placing stop-loss and take-profit orders and controlling position sizes.

Consistency: A trading strategy should be repeatable and consistent, with principles that can be applied to diverse market conditions.

Flexibility: A trading strategy should be adaptable enough to changes in market conditions and fresh information.

Backtesting and Optimizing a Trading Strategy

Once you've created a trading strategy, you should test it against historical data to determine how it would have fared in the past. This is referred to as backtesting.

Backtesting is the process of applying a trading strategy to previous data and analyzing its performance with metrics such as profit and loss, win rate, and drawdown. This helps you to spot any flaws in the approach and make changes before putting real money at risk in the markets.

Optimizing a trading strategy entail making changes to the strategy depending on the results of backtesting. This can include changing the strategy's entry and exit rules, updating risk management parameters, or adding additional indicators or filters.

Backtesting and optimizing a trading strategy can assist to enhance its performance, but it is not a guarantee of future success. Market conditions can shift quickly, and past success does not always predict future outcomes.

A successful trading strategy necessitates careful consideration of your trading style, as well as critical characteristics of a successful strategy such as clear entry and exit criteria, risk management, consistency, and adaptability.

Pros & Cons of Backtesting

Pros of Backtesting

- Identifying Weaknesses: Backtesting can help to identify weaknesses in a trading strategy that may not be apparent in live trading. By testing the strategy on historical data, traders can see how it would have performed in different market conditions and identify any patterns or trends that may affect its performance.

- Refining the Strategy: Once weaknesses have been identified, traders can refine their strategy by making adjustments based on the backtesting results.

  This can include tweaking entry and exit rules, adjusting risk management parameters, or adding new indicators or filters to the strategy.

- Increasing Confidence: Backtesting can boost a trader's confidence in their approach by demonstrating its past performance. This can assist in lowering the emotional impact of trading decisions and improving overall trading discipline.

Cons of Backtesting:

- Over-Optimization: Over-optimization is one of the most serious risks of backtesting, where a trader makes too many tweaks to their strategy based on prior performance, resulting in a system that is too complex and may not function in live trading.

- Limited Market Data: Backtesting relies on previous market data, which may or may not be reflective of current market conditions. As a result, a strategy that was optimized for previous market conditions may no longer function in the current market.

- Emotionless Trading: Backtesting does not take into account the emotional impact of trading decisions, which can have a significant impact on a trader's performance. Traders in live trading may make decisions based on fear or greed, which can lead to bad trading results.

So, what I'm I saying? Backtesting can help you improve your trading strategies and boost your confidence in your approach. It can aid in identifying flaws and making changes.

You must, however, be cautious not to over-optimize your strategies and be conscious of the limitations of past data.

Now, despite the cons, backtesting is extremely important and can not be overlooked. There are so many software and tool out there that can help you easily backtest your strategies. And example is FX Replay. You can check it out here: app.fxreplay.com.

Another option would be to backtest on Tradingview using the replay mode.

Keep in mind that past performance does not guarantee future success. As a trader you can establish effective trading methods that lead to long-term profits with the appropriate attitude and a dedication to constant learning and improvement.

Chapter 10

Smart Money Concept

HOW TO TRADE LIKE THE BANKS

The banks are some of the world's largest and most successful traders. They have an army of analysts and traders working around the clock to ensure they are always ahead of the game. So, how do they do it?

It pays to know how big players trade if you're looking to get an edge in the markets. In this lesson, we'll explore the so-called "smart money" concept and show you how you can start trading like the banks.

THE CONCEPT

In the world of trading, there is a lot of "talk" about the so-called "smart money. "This is the group of professional traders and investors seen as the biggest and smartest players.

The smart money concept is based on the idea that a group of professional traders and investors have access to information that the general public does not. This information gives them an edge in the market, so they can make better investment decisions.

"Smart Money" is the capital that has been invested in the market by institutions, and other financial experts. This collective power of large amounts of money that influence and move financial markets is referred to as "Smart Money".

"Smart Money Trading" or **"Institutional Trading"** is when retail traders use institutional trading techniques and strategies when trading. The driving force behind smart money is the central bank.

That is why you hear people say, "trade like the banks". Institutional investors are thought to have superior investing methods that differ from those of retail investors, giving Smart Money a higher chance of success.

Interbank (AKA Smart Money) market vs Retail market

The **Interbank Market** is the top-tier foreign exchange market where the smart money or the biggest players in the game trade currencies. It is made up of institutional investors, central banks, and other financial institutions or specialists.

They are the ones who provide the Bid and Ask values for each currency pair. No wonder they are called the **"Market Makers".** They own the game. They have access to more information, make trades faster, and have more capital.

The **"Retail Market"** also known as the herd, is made up of small financial institutions including forex brokers, banks, hedge funds, speculators, and day traders. Basically, whatever isn't part of the interbank market qualifies as the retail market. Retail traders don't own the game.

All we do is play the game and this is why it's important to learn how the institutions behave and places their orders so that we can use these insights when trading our own strategy.

The key to successful trading is to find ways to get an edge over the banks. One way to do this is by understanding how they operate and what their goals are. Once you know this, you can use their tactics against them.

Stop Hunting

The institutions are aware that due to the high degree of leverage involved in trading, both major and small traders frequently utilize stop and stop-limit orders to avoid margin calls and automatically lock in profits.

So, the big boys would use the stop hunting tactic (which involves driving an asset's price to a level where many traders have decided to set their stop-loss orders) in an effort to discourage some traders from holding their positions or completely force them out of their trade.

When stop losses are simultaneously triggered it can cause substantial volatility moves. They'll steer you in one direction, manipulate the market to get you confused, and then take your position before continuing in their original direction.

The "algorithm" know where people are likely to place their stop loss, and this is why some traders use "Mental Stop Loss".

When it comes to trading, the banks are the smart money. They have deep pockets and can weather any storm. You must be prepared to lose if you want to trade like the banks too. After all, they know that people are learning how to trade like them.

The banks don't get emotional about their trades. They have a plan, and they stick to it. If you want to be successful, you need to do the same.

The key to trading like the banks is always preparing for the worst. That way, when the markets turn against you, you won't panic and sell at a loss.

If you can stick to your plan and stay calm when the markets are losing (whether you are trading smart money or not), you'll be on your way to success.

Order Flow & Liquidity

If you're looking to trade like the banks, it's important to understand order flow. Order flow is the net flow of buy and sells orders in the market.

Order flow trading is a sort of study that involves tracking the flow of trading orders and their impact on the price. Banks are always the biggest players in the market, so they hugely impact order flow.

Order flow trading will give you insight regarding buy and sell orders, liquidity flow, momentum, momentum exhaustion, buyers and sellers who are trapped, and stop hunts.

Another key to trading like the banks is to trade with the flow of order flow. When there's more buying than selling, prices will go up. When there's more selling than buying, prices will go down.

Following the order flow, you can trade like the banks and profit from their moves. When the order flow is drying off it may be a sign that a reversal is about to start.

How does the saying go? "The trend is your friend." This is especially true when it comes to trading. The market is constantly changing, and you'll be left behind if you don't stay ahead of the curve.

This would involve having a set of rules and strategies in order to get in the market when the institutions are also placing their order.

The big mistake a lot of traders make is that they think that "smart money trading" automatically means 'counter-trend trading.' This is not correct because you can trade like the banks while still trading with the trend. (You will learn about this in the next lesson).

Liquidity Models

The Liquidity Model is an important tool for banks as it allows them to identify and quantify the risks they are exposed to. It is also useful for regulators as it provides a framework for assessing the resilience of financial institutions to potential liquidity shocks.

The model comprises three components:

1. The wholesale funding model: The wholesale funding model estimates the amount of wholesale funding required to meet a given level of stressed outflows.

2. The retail funding model: The retail funding model estimates the number of retail deposits required to meet a given level of stressed outflows.

3. The market-based liquidity model: The market-based liquidity model estimates the number of securities that would need to be sold to meet a given level of stressed outflows.

The institutions tend to trade in large volumes, which can significantly impact market prices. So, what does all this mean for the average trader? If you're looking to trade like smart money, you need to know what these large investors are doing.

One way to keep track of smart money is to watch for unusual market movements. For example, if you see a sudden spike in volume or price movement in the market, this could indicate that smart money is behind it.

Another thing to look for is trades that are out of the norm. If you see a trade that doesn't seem to make sense from a fundamental standpoint, then it could be smart money. They are the ones who are always in the know and always ahead of the game. They have access to the information we don't have and use it to their advantage.

To be a successful trader, you must start thinking like the banks. What information do they have that you don't? How can you get your hands on that information?

It's not impossible, but it will take some work. Start by reading up on the latest news and economic reports. Pay attention to what the banks are saying and doing. And most importantly, don't be afraid to ask questions.

The more you know, the better equipped you'll be to make smart trades that will put you ahead of the pack.

Here are some tips:

1. Be patient. The banks are patient traders. They don't make rash decisions; they wait for the perfect opportunity.

2. Be disciplined. The banks have a strict trading discipline. They stick to their rules and don't let emotions influence their decisions.

3. Be informed. The banks have access to information that most retail traders don't. They use this information to their advantage.

4. Be patient. This one is worth repeating. The banks are patient traders. They don't make rash decisions; they wait for the perfect opportunity.

In the next lesson, you will learn one of the most commonly known and used smart money trading strategies.

Chapter 11

The Powerful Smart Money Strategy

Now let's talk about **Smart Money - OB Strategy**. Before we do, let's remind ourselves what 'Smart Money' is.

Smart Money: This is the capital that is under the management of institutional investors, central banks, market experts, funds, and other financial experts. Smart Money

Trading or Institutional Trading is usually more accurate than retail market trading. This is because they are the big boys and have a strong influence on the financial market and so we want to trade like them.

Smart Money: Order Block & Breaker Block

If you're looking to trade like the banks, it's important to understand how they operate. One key concept is ordered block trading.

Order block trading is when the banks place orders for large blocks of shares at a certain price. This is usually the best available price, and it's typically done to quickly fill a large order.

The banks will often place these orders ahead of time and wait for the market to move to their desired price. They'll execute their order and fill their block when the market reaches their price.

This type of trading allows the banks to get the best possible price for their large orders, which retail traders can also take advantage of.

If you see a large order is placed at a certain price, the bank is likely trying to fill a larger order, and you may be able to get in on the action by placing your order at that same price in combination with a candlesticks pattern.

If you can learn to trade like the banks, you'll be in a much better position to make money in the markets.

Ok enough Janie! Let's get into the strategy.
The first thing we will need to do is to go on a higher timeframe (H4 or 1D timeframe, I prefer H4) and identify the structure. Is the market making higher highs (HH) and higher lows (HL)? Then we are in an uptrend.

Or is the market making lower lows (LL) and lower highs (LH)? Then you are in a downtrend. It's important that we see at least 2 or 3 break of structures or series or HH/HL for uptrend and LL/LH for a downtrend.

Once we've identified the market structure on the H4, we will need to write it down. For example, 'H4 is in an uptrend.' After we've identified the trend, we grab our horizontal line or trend line drawing tool and place it on the most recent High and low, only!

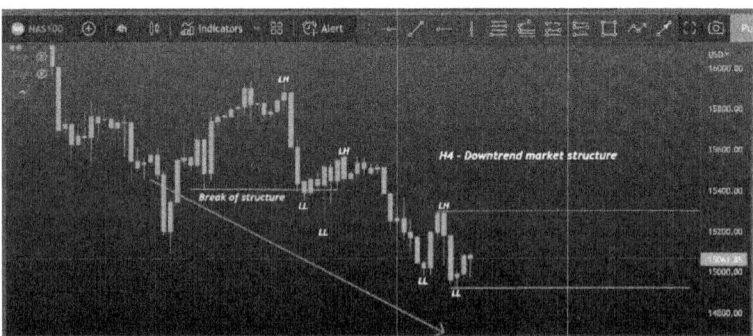

Next, we go down to the H1 timeframe and also identify the structure and also write it down. We don't necessarily have to plot or draw the horizontal line or trend line drawing tool as we did on the H4, but what is important is that the structure should be the same as the H4 timeframe which in this case is a downtrend as seen in the image.

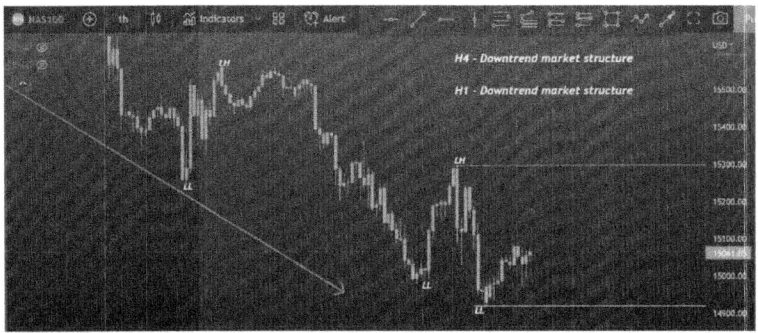

The next step would be to go down to our entry timeframe and this could be 5Mins or 15Mins timeframe, but I prefer the 15Mins timeframe. On the 15Mins we'll need the market or price to be heading towards the opposite trend direction of the higher timeframes.

So, for example, if the H4 and H1 structures are bearish, we need the 15Mins to be bullish. In most cases it is actually heading to an order block where it can create a swing, reject from, and continue in the direction of the higher timeframe... so we let it ride to it.

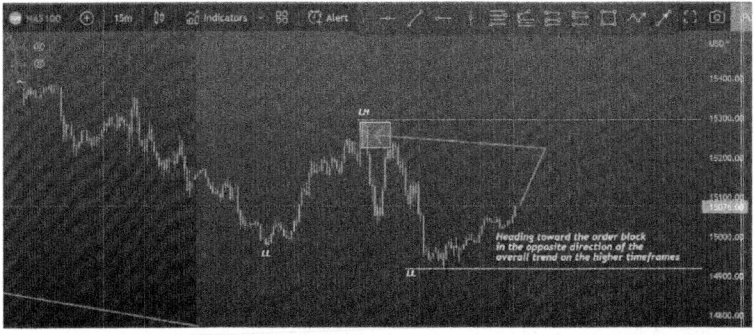

A key point to keep in mind is that if the opposite trend movement on the 15Mins breaks the horizontal line, we cancel the trade and look for another setup. Also, keep in mind that the LL and LH you see on the 15Mins and H1 timeframes are the same ones on the H4 timeframe.

I decided not to move them so you can see what they actually look like on a lower timeframe.

Back to the strategy... Once we see that the price is indeed heading towards the 15 Mins order block, we can set a buy/sell limit order or buy/sell stop order right at the body (not the wick) of the order block close to the current price.

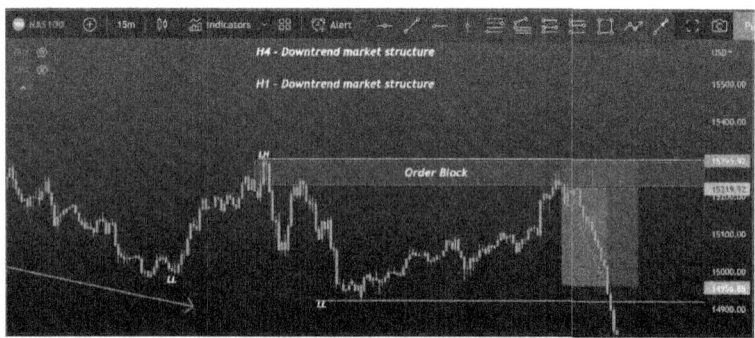

As we've seen in the image above, we will set our stop-loss at the other end of the order block. We set or take profit at the next order block in the direction of the higher timeframe trend or set your preferred risk-to-reward ratio.

If you would like to swing the trade and hold for a longer time, then your profit target could be the next order block on any of the higher time frames, but please make sure to secure some profit as you go.

This strategy requires patience which will in turn reward you due to its high win rate. Now go on your chart and find minimum examples (1 uptrend and 1 downtrend) and examine how this strategy played out. Then the forward test.

Now that we've delved into strategies and underlined the value of backtesting, it's time to address the real game-changer in your trading journey - "Trading Psychology" and the art of "Staying Disciplined".

Intrigued? Let's dive right in!

Chapter 12

Stay Disciplined

To me, Discipline is not just a trait you hope to have, but rather a practice that you hone and refine every single day.

"Discipline is the ability to act in a consistent and ordered manner in order to accomplish positive results."

Consider discipline as your personal navigation system, guiding you through the landscape of trading. It propels you to continually execute necessary tasks, even when they may seem tedious or uninteresting.

This perseverance is key to producing positive results and it fast-tracks your progression towards your trading objectives, despite the occasional discomfort it may bring.

Discipline in trading takes on various shapes. One of these is the discipline of strictly adhering to your trading plan. This is a set of guidelines you've devised based on your risk tolerance, trading capital, and overall market approach.

This plan is your guide, and deviating from it could take you into uncharted territory, subjecting you to undue risk.

Another facet of discipline is emotional control. The financial market is a roller coaster of highs and lows. It can be tempting to let emotions, such as fear or greed, drive your decisions.

But disciplined traders understand that emotional reactions often lead to mistakes. Instead, they strive to maintain a level head, making decisions based on careful analysis rather than transient feelings.

Discipline also involves setting and respecting stop-loss orders.

These are pre-determined levels at which you'll exit a trade to limit your losses. It's tempting to ignore these levels when you're in the heat of the moment, hoping that a losing trade will turn around. But doing so is a breach of discipline that could cost you significantly.

Did you know that disciplined traders are committed to ongoing learning? The financial market is dynamic and continually evolving. Yesterday's successful approach may not work today.

It is necessary to keep pace with the latest market trends, news, and technologies. This could involve reading financial news, participating in webinars, or signing up for advanced trading courses.

Discipline is about taking responsibility for your actions. When a trade goes wrong, it's easy to blame market volatility, bad luck, or faulty advice. But disciplined traders own their mistakes.

They understand that each loss is a learning opportunity, a chance to refine their strategy and grow as a trader.

So what I'm I saying? Discipline is the bedrock upon which successful trading strategies are built. It's a trait that's cultivated over time, not something you acquire overnight. It's about making smart decisions consistently, sticking to your plan, managing your emotions, and constantly striving to learn and improve.

And remember, in the financial market, discipline is not just an option - it's a prerequisite for success.

Key Components of Trading Psychology

EMOTIONAL CONTROL

Emotions are integral to human behavior, but in trading, they can lead to hasty decisions. Managing emotions is crucial to maintaining a clear mind and making rational trading decisions.

Common emotions experienced by traders: Traders often grapple with feelings like fear, greed, regret, and overconfidence. These emotions, if not managed well, can cloud judgment and lead to poor trading outcomes.

Various techniques can be employed for emotional control, such as deep breathing exercises, meditation, and maintaining a healthy work-life balance. It's also beneficial to follow a strict trading plan and practice discipline.

DISCIPLINE AND CONSISTENCY

Discipline is the foundation of successful trading. It involves sticking to your trading plan, managing risk effectively, and staying patient in the face of market volatility.

Consistency can be maintained by setting a regular trading schedule, continually reviewing and refining your strategy, and staying updated with market trends.

Distractions, fear of missing out, and overtrading are common obstacles. Overcoming these requires focus, emotional control, and a thorough understanding of one's trading strategy.

RISK MANAGEMENT

Risk management is key to preserving your trading capital. It involves setting appropriate stop-loss and take-profit levels and diversifying your portfolio.

Striking a balance between risk and reward is crucial. This involves understanding the potential downside of each trade and ensuring the potential upside justifies the risk.

Some techniques include setting appropriate leverage levels, using protective stops, and regularly reviewing your risk management strategy.

COGNITIVE BIASES IN TRADING

Cognitive biases are mental shortcuts or patterns of thinking that can lead to irrational decisions and, in trading, potential losses.

Common biases affecting traders:

Confirmation bias: Traders may unconsciously seek out information that supports their existing beliefs while ignoring contradictory evidence.

Overconfidence bias: Traders may overestimate their abilities or the accuracy of their predictions, leading to excessive risk-taking.

Loss aversion: Traders may be more inclined to avoid losses than to seek gains, which can lead to poor decision-making.

Anchoring bias: Traders may rely heavily on the first piece of information they encounter (the "anchor") when making decisions.

Developing A Winning Trader Mindset

Having a clear and measurable objective in mind helps provide direction and creates a sense of purpose in what can often be a volatile and chaotic environment.

With time-bound targets, you foster motivation and maintain focus, creating a structured framework within which you can progress.

What distinguishes successful traders from the rest is their ability to approach trading with a growth mindset.

They understand that trading is not simply about inherent talent or skill. Instead, it's a journey of constant learning, refining strategies, and cultivating the intelligence needed to navigate the complex financial markets.

A growth mindset inspires traders to treat every mistake as a learning opportunity and every challenge as a potential avenue for growth. It's this ability to learn from their own missteps that propels their journey towards becoming adept traders.

The journey, though, is never a smooth sail. Setbacks and losses are as much a part of trading as gains and victories. It's here that resilience plays a pivotal role.

Successful traders are not just those who can strategize well, but also those who can endure the occasional storm.

They cultivate resilience by adopting a positive attitude, even in the face of adversity.

They practice stress management techniques to stay composed during volatile market conditions and rely on their robust support network to keep them grounded. Their ability to bounce back from losses and setbacks is a testament to their mental strength and tenacity.

Along with resilience, another crucial aspect of mastering trading is self-reflection. Traders who make time to pause, assess, and reflect on their actions, decisions, and outcomes can derive profound insights from this introspection.

They scrutinize their trading decisions and identify areas where they can improve. This process of self-reflection not only allows them to fine-tune their trading strategy but also to learn from past mistakes and prevent them from repeating the same errors in the future.

This continuous cycle of action, reflection, learning, and improvement is integral to the journey of becoming a successful trader.

The one thing that every successful trader will tell you is that achieving success in trading isn't an overnight affair. It requires setting realistic goals, nurturing a growth mindset, building resilience, and committing to regular self-reflection and learning.

This holistic approach allows traders to constantly evolve, adapt, and thrive in the dynamic world of trading.

Here are some points to keep in mind:

- Craft your currency trading strategy with the understanding that it's a marathon, not a sprint. Developing the necessary skills will require time and dedication.

- Let patience be your constant companion on this journey. It's not just about waiting for the perfect trading opportunity, but also about timing your entries and exits precisely.

- Discipline isn't merely doing what's needed; it's about doing it consistently. This involves:
1. Conducting rigorous research and chart analysis before each trading day or week.
2. Testing and adjusting your strategies as market conditions evolve.
3. Avoiding impulsive and revenge trading, which can lead to significant account losses.

- Adhere to the golden rule: Don't let your losses grow excessively large or cut your profits too soon.

- Resist the Fear Of Missing Out (FOMO) that might push you into trades prematurely or without meeting your established trading rules and criteria. At the same time, don't just sit idly by, watching the markets move while waiting for your ideal opportunity.

- Make it a habit to maintain and regularly review a trade journal. Despite not being popular among many newcomers, it's a powerful learning tool in your trading toolkit.

- Work on developing the patience and discipline necessary for making wise trading decisions. It may be a challenging task, akin to climbing a steep mountain, but the view from the top is worth every tough step.

- Above all else, ensure that you have a well-thought-out trading plan and strategy.

Your primary goal is to master the art of making sound trading decisions, and most importantly, to persist! It's crucial to approach your trading career like a long-distance race, not a 100-meter dash.

Trading is far from a lottery. It's a game of strategy and patience, not a whirlwind path to overnight riches.

If you stay patient, disciplined, and dedicated, you'll likely see your initial results as a novice trader gradually improve.

Good trade opportunities are like buses - another one will be along soon. There's no need to gamble on risky trades that could derail your progress towards your goals. Instead, stick to your best trade setups and ideas.

If your setups don't align during the current trading session, remember, tomorrow brings a new day and a fresh opportunity. There's always another trade on the horizon, as long as currencies continue to exchange hands globally.

Tips for Mastering the Mental Game of Trading

To master the mental game of trading, traders need to understand and manage their emotions and psychological biases. Here are some practical tips to help traders improve their trading psychology:

Keep a Trading Journal

Keeping a trading journal is an effective way to track your progress, identify patterns, and reflect on your trading decisions. It's also a great tool for holding yourself accountable and staying disciplined.

To get insights into their decision-making process, traders can record their transactions, emotions, and thoughts before, during, and after the trade.

Traders can discover their strengths and limitations and develop tactics to enhance their trading psychology by analyzing their journal.

Practice Mindfulness

In the face of uncertainty and volatility, mindfulness is a strategy that can help you as a traders stay focused and calm.

Traders can learn to monitor their thoughts and emotions without judgment and avoid impulsive and irrational decision-making by practicing mindfulness.

Deep breathing and visualization are two mindfulness practices that can assist traders reduce stress and anxiety while also improving their trading performance.

Develop a Trading Plan
Developing a trading plan can help traders stay disciplined and avoid emotional biases. A trading plan should include entry and exit rules, risk management strategies, and guidelines for managing emotions.

Traders should stick to their trading plan and avoid deviating from it based on emotions or impulse.

Manage Risk
Risk management is an essential component of successful trading and can help traders avoid emotional biases. Traders should limit their risk exposure and use stop-loss orders to minimize losses. They should also diversify their portfolio and avoid putting all their eggs in one basket.

Take Breaks
Trading can be stressful, and traders need to take breaks to manage their emotions and avoid burnout. Traders should take regular breaks to recharge and refocus. They should also avoid trading when they are tired, hungry, or stressed, as these factors can affect their decision-making.

Seek Support

Trading can be a lonely and isolating activity, and traders need to seek support from other traders, mentors, or therapists. Joining a trading community can provide traders with a support system and help them learn from other traders' experiences.

Traders can also seek professional help if they are struggling with emotional issues that affect their trading performance.

Continuous Education and Skill Development

The financial markets are dynamic and ever-changing. Continuous learning is essential to stay updated with market trends, new trading technologies, and advanced trading strategies.

This could involve reading financial news, attending webinars, or enrolling in advanced trading courses.

Mastering the mental game of trading is crucial for achieving consistent profits in financial markets. Traders need to understand and manage their emotions and psychological biases to make rational decisions and avoid impulsive and irrational behavior.

By keeping a trading journal, practicing mindfulness, developing a trading plan, managing risk, taking breaks, and seeking support, traders can improve their trading psychology and achieve long-term success in financial markets.

Chapter 13

Forex Trading for Day Traders

Day trading is a popular approach to Forex trading that involves opening and closing positions within the same trading day. Day traders are known for their ability to capitalize on short-term price movements in the Forex market, which can yield significant profits if done correctly.

In this chapter, we will explore the ins and outs of day trading in Forex, including strategies, techniques, and tips for success.

What is Day Trading?

Day trading is a Forex trading style that involves buying and selling currency pairs within the same trading day. This means that all positions are closed before the market closes for the day, regardless of whether they are profitable or not.

Day traders typically use technical analysis to identify short-term price movements in the market, which they can capitalize on for quick profits.

Day Trading Strategies and Techniques

There are several day trading strategies that traders use to make profits in the Forex market. These strategies can vary depending on the trader's preferences, risk tolerance, and market conditions. Here are some popular day trading strategies and techniques:

Scalping - This strategy involves making multiple trades throughout the day, aiming to capture small profits from each trade. Scalping requires traders to enter and exit positions quickly, as the profit potential from each trade is small.

Breakout trading - This strategy involves identifying key levels of support and resistance in the market, and entering positions when the price breaks out of these levels. Breakout trading can be a high-risk strategy, as false breakouts can result in significant losses.

Trend following - This strategy involves identifying the direction of the prevailing trend in the market and entering positions in the same direction. Trend following can be a profitable strategy, as long as traders are able to correctly identify the trend and enter positions at the right time.

News trading - This strategy involves trading based on news events that can affect the Forex market. News traders typically look for high-impact news releases that can cause significant price movements in the market.

Day Trading Tips and Tricks

Day trading can be a challenging and high-risk trading style, but there are several tips and tricks that traders can use to improve their chances of success. Here are some tips and tricks for day traders:

Have a plan - Before entering any trades, day traders should have a clear plan in place that outlines their entry and exit strategies, risk management approach, and profit targets.

Use stop-loss orders - Stop-loss orders can help traders limit their losses in case the market moves against them. Traders should always use stop-loss orders to protect their capital.

Avoid overtrading - Overtrading can lead to significant losses and burnout. Day traders should stick to their trading plan and only enter trades when they meet their criteria.

Stay informed - Day traders should stay up to date on market news, economic data releases, and other factors that can affect the Forex market. This can help them make more informed trading decisions.

Practice and refine your strategy - Day trading requires practice and patience. Traders should take the time to practice their strategies on a demo account before trading with real money. They should also continuously refine their strategy based on their performance and market conditions.

So, day trading can really be a profitable trading style if done correctly. You should use a combination of strategies, techniques, and tips to increase their chances of success.

However, day trading can also be high-risk, and traders should always approach it with caution and a solid risk management plan.

Chapter 14

Forex Trading for Swing Traders

Swing trading is a popular trading method whereby trades are held for a short amount of time than day trading, often a few days to a few weeks.

Swing trading aims to capitalize on short-term price changes within the framework of a longer-term trend. In this chapter, we will discuss swing trading in detail, including its strategies, techniques, and tips.

What is Swing Trading?

Swing trading is a trading style that seeks to capture short-term price movements within the context of a longer-term trend. Swing traders use technical analysis to identify key levels of support and resistance, and they enter and exit positions based on price action signals.

Swing traders, as opposed to day traders, maintain their positions for a few days to a few weeks, depending on market conditions and their trading technique.

Swing Trading Strategies and Techniques

Swing traders use a variety of trading strategies and techniques to identify and capture short-term price movements. Some of the most common swing trading tactics are as follows:

Trend Trading: is a swing trading method that involves identifying and trading in the direction of a dominant trend. Traders use technical indicators such as moving averages, trend lines, and price channels to identify the direction of the trend and enter trades in the direction of the trend.

Breakout Trading: Breakout trading is a swing trading strategy that involves identifying key levels of support and resistance and entering trades when the price breaks out of these levels.

The RSI (Relative Strength Index) is a great indicator for confirming a breakout. Another option would be to use a trendline as I have shown in the image below. You will need to wait for price to breaks out of the trendline first.

A break out of the sideway / ranging market, followed by a mini pullback, and then a drop in price

dingView

Pullback Trading: Pullback trading is a swing trading strategy that involves entering trades after a retracement in the price. Traders use technical indicators such as Fibonacci retracements and moving averages to identify potential retracement levels and enter trades when the price retraces to these levels.

After an impulsive move, a trader plots their Fib tool, and wait for it to retrace.

After an impulsive move, a trader plots their Fib tool, and wait for it to retrace to one of these levels. Just keep in mind that the stronger the initial impulsive move, the less likelihood that it would have a deep retracement.

Price Action Trading: Price action trading is trading strategy that involves analyzing the price action of the market to identify key levels of support and resistance and enter trades based on price action signals such as pin bars, inside bars, and engulfing bars.

Swing Trading Tips and Tricks

Here are some swing trading tips to help you enhance your trading performance:

1. Use a Trading Plan: Swing traders should have a clear trading strategy, risk management guidelines, and trading objectives. A trading plan helps traders to stay disciplined and focused and reduces the chances of emotional trading decisions.

2. Keep an Eye on the News: Swing traders should stay informed about the news and economic events that can affect the market. News events such as central bank announcements, economic data releases, and geopolitical events can cause significant volatility in the market and affect trading positions.

3. Use Stop Losses: Stop losses are essential risk management tools that help traders to limit their losses in case the market moves against their positions. Swing traders should use stop losses to protect their trading capital and reduce the risk of significant losses.

4. Keep a Trading Journal: Swing traders should keep a trading journal to record their trades, analyze their performance, and identify areas for improvement. A trading journal helps traders to learn from their mistakes and refine their trading strategies over time.

Swing trading is a popular trading style that can be profitable if done correctly. This is actually one of my favorites. Swing traders use both fundamental and technical analysis to identify short-term price movements within the context of a longer-term trend.

They use a variety of trading strategies and techniques to enter and exit trades based on price action signals.

To be a successful swing trader, traders should have a well-defined trading plan, use risk management tools such as stop losses, stay informed about the news, and keep a trading journal to track their performance.

Chapter 15

Forex Trading for Long-Term Investors

You're probably conversant with stocks and bonds. But have you ever really considered the potential advantages of including Forex trading into your investment strategy? Well let's talk about it while highlighting the advantages, risks, and methods for trading currencies effectively.

As mentioned before, Forex trading involves buying and selling different currencies, and can be done right from your living room. It is the world's largest and most liquid financial market. Those who Participate in the currency market are the financial institutions, central banks, multinational enterprises, and individual investors.

With its high liquidity, 24-hour market operation, and ease of access through online trading platforms, Forex offers unique opportunities for long-term investors. But are there any real benefits?

Benefits of Forex Trading for Long-term Investors

- Diversification: Forex trading allows investors to diversify their portfolios by gaining exposure to various international economies. By investing in different currencies, long-term investors can hedge against regional risks and enhance their overall returns.

- Lower transaction costs: Forex trading typically has lower transaction costs when compared to stocks or bonds, which makes it a better option for long-term some investors.

- Interest rate differentials: By transacting in currencies with higher interest rates, long-term investors can profit from interest rate differentials.

- Inflation hedge: Forex trading can serve as a hedge against inflation, particularly in countries with high inflation rates, by investing in currencies with stronger economies and lower inflation.

Risks Involved in Forex Trading

Currency risk: Currency risk is a possibility that a currency's value will fall relative to other currencies, reducing investment returns.

Leverage risk: The use of borrowed money to increase the potential returns of an investment, which can also magnify losses.

Political risk: A nation's currency value may change immediately due to changes in its political situation.

Economic risk: Currency values can be influenced by shifts in inflation, interest rates, and economic growth.

Liquidity risk: The risk of not being able to easily turn an investment into cash without suffering a considerable loss in value.

Forex Trading Strategies for Long-Term Investors

There are several strategies for long term investing, hut here 3 types you can keep in mind.

Fundamental analysis: Long-term investors should concentrate on understanding the fundamental economic factors that influence currency prices, like inflation, interest rate, and GDP growth.

By analyzing these factors, investors can identify long-term trends to enter or exit a trade.

Carry trade strategy: So, what happens here is that a trader will borrow money in a low-interest-rate currency and then invest it in a high-interest-rate currency.

You can profit from the difference in interest rates between the two currencies, as well as potential gain in the higher-yielding currency.

Diversification and portfolio allocation: Long-term investors should allocate a portion of their portfolio to Forex trading to achieve diversification and potentially enhance overall returns. If you can take the time to carefully select a mix of currencies, you as an investor can mitigate risk and take advantage of global economic trends.

Tips for Successful Forex Trading

1. Develop a trading plan. Set clear investment objectives, risk tolerance levels, and outline a strategy to achieve them.
2. Choose a reputable Forex broker. Select a broker with a solid reputation, strong regulatory oversight, and competitive pricing.
3. Stay informed. Keep up to date with global economic news and events that may impact currency values.
4. Manage risk. Implement stop-loss orders, limit orders, and position sizing to manage risk effectively.
5. Practice patience and discipline. Successful long-term Forex trading requires patience, discipline, and a consistent approach.

Forex trading offers unique opportunities for long-term investors looking to diversify their portfolios and take advantage.

Chapter 16

Prop Firms, Should You Use Them?

In the dynamic world of Forex trading, traders are constantly seeking new avenues to enhance their strategies. One option that has gained popularity is utilizing proprietary trading firms, also known as prop firms, for Forex trading.

These firms offer traders access to substantial capital, advanced tools, and a supportive community. However, before deciding whether to engage with prop firms, it is essential to examine the advantages and disadvantages associated with this approach.

In this chapter, we will delve into the factors to consider when using prop firms for Forex trading.

Advantages of Proprietary Trading Firms

Increased Capital and Leverage

Prop firms provide traders with access to significant capital and leverage. This allows traders to execute larger trades and potentially generate higher profits compared to individual trading.

The availability of increased leverage enables traders to capitalize on even minor market movements.

Advanced Trading Tools and Technology

Proprietary trading firms are renowned for their state-of-the-art trading infrastructure and advanced technology. Traders benefit from sophisticated trading platforms, real-time market data, and advanced analytics.

These resources empower traders to make well-informed decisions, execute trades efficiently, and stay competitive.

Risk Management and Supportive Community

Forex trading can be a solitary pursuit, but prop firms offer a supportive community of experienced traders. These firms often provide risk management training and support, allowing traders to benefit from shared insights and mentorship.

Additionally, prop firms may allocate risk capital to traders, reducing personal risk and enabling traders to focus on their trading strategies.

Disadvantages of Proprietary Trading Firms

Profit-Sharing and Performance Expectations

Prop firms typically operate on a profit-sharing model, where traders are required to share a portion of their profits with the firm. This reduces traders' overall earnings.

Moreover, prop firms often set high performance targets for traders to meet. These expectations can create pressure and stress, potentially impacting a trader's decision-making process and overall performance.

Losses and Risk Exposure

While prop firms offer the potential for amplified profits, they also increase the risk exposure. Traders must recognize that losses are magnified as well, and in some cases, they may be responsible for covering a portion of these losses.

Managing risk becomes crucial when trading with prop firms to protect capital and mitigate potential losses.

Limited Autonomy and Trading Restrictions

Trading through prop firms often entails adhering to predefined rules and guidelines set by the firm. This may limit a trader's autonomy to implement their own unique trading strategies or explore specific markets and instruments.

Traders who prefer a more individualistic approach may find this lack of flexibility restrictive.

Making an Informed Decision

Deciding whether to engage with prop firms for Forex trading requires careful consideration of personal circumstances and goals.

Evaluate your trading style, risk tolerance, and the resources and community support offered by prop firms.

Consider the advantages and disadvantages outlined in this chapter so that you can make decisions that aligns with your individual needs and aspirations.

Conclusion

Alright, let's conclude. If you are still reading, Congrats! You've done an amazing job investing in yourself through learning. You see, trading the financial markets can be a little complex and challenging and requires a great deal of skill and knowledge to navigate successfully.

This book has provided a comprehensive guide for beginners to get started in Forex trading. Here are some of the important points to remember:

1. So, first things first, it is inevitable to understand the fundamentals of Forex trading, such as market structure and trading advantages and disadvantages. To be honest, it'll be hard for you to make good trading decisions without this foundation.

2. Secondly, mastering the essential trading tools is crucial for effective trading. Understanding trading platforms, different types of trading charts, and indicators, and setting up a trading account is necessary.

3. Thirdly, both fundamental and technical analysis are important in Forex trading. Fundamental analysis helps you understand the economic indicators that affect the market, while technical analysis helps you identify trends and patterns in price movements.

4. Fourthly, risk management is crucial in Forex trading. It is important to set up stop loss & take profit orders and calculate position sizes to minimize risks.

5. Fifthly, developing a trading strategy is an essential part of Forex trading. When you take the time to backtest and optimize your trading strategies, you'll better understand the market as well as your trading style, so that you can make informed decisions.

6. Sixthly, understanding the psychological aspect of trading and controlling emotions is important in Forex trading. Common trading emotions like fear and greed can cloud your judgment, and developing a trader's mindset is crucial.

7. Seventhly, Forex trading offers different trading styles like day trading, swing trading, and long-term trading. You'll need to use specific approach and technique for each trading style or strategy, and it is imperative to select the one that best complements your trading style.

8. Lastly, continuous learning and practice are crucial to becoming a successful Forex trader. The market is constantly evolving, and being current on new trends and strategies is essential for adapting to market changes. Practice, practice! This is necessary to improve your trading abilities.

Forex trading is a dynamic and exciting industry that provides traders with plenty of options. It is, however, a difficult market that requires a good knowledge and experience to succeed.

You can improve your chances of being a good Forex trader by mastering the basics, using necessary trading tools, building a trading strategy and system, and constantly learning and practicing.

Take advantage of the free resources and learning platforms like the one on Jeivestor.com website and YouTube channel.

Remember that becoming a great trader requires time, effort, and discipline, but the benefits can be tremendous.

THANK YOU!

Free resources:

www.jeivestor.com

www.youtube.com/@Jeivestor

To access the Skilled Trading Masterclass course, go here:

https://bit.ly/44lqDFd

ABOUT THE AUTHOR

Hi there, I am happy you made it this far and I hope you enjoyed the book. I am the CEO of Jeivestor. I am a businesswoman, an investor, a mentor, a writer, and a content creator. I am passionate about all things finance, budgeting and investing.

I love investing not just in properties and assets, but most importantly, in people. It is a greater asset to own. I love the word "Simple" because I believe this is how everyone should see life and things around them.

My goal is to continue inspiring and helping as much people as I can.

Printed in Great Britain
by Amazon